DIANA, PRINCESS OF WALES

Recent Titles in Greenwood Biographies

Steven Spielberg: A Biography
Kathi Jackson

Madonna: A Biography
Mary Cross

Jackie Robinson: A Biography
Mary Kay Linge

Bob Marley: A Biography
David V. Moskowitz

Sitting Bull: A Biography
Edward J. Rielly

Eleanor Roosevelt: A Biography
Cynthia M. Harris

Jesse Owens: A Biography
Jacqueline Edmondson

The Notorious B.I.G.: A Biography
Holly Lang

Hillary Clinton: A Biography
Dena B. Levy and Nicole R. Krassas

Johnny Depp: A Biography
Michael Blitz

Judy Blume: A Biography
Kathleen Tracy

Nelson Mandela: A Biography
Peter Limb

Lebron James: A Biography
Lew Freedman

DIANA, PRINCESS OF WALES

A Biography

Martin Gitlin

GREENWOOD BIOGRAPHIES

GREENWOOD PRESS
WESTPORT, CONNECTICUT • LONDON

Library of Congress Cataloging-in-Publication Data

Gitlin, Marty.
   Diana, Princess of Wales : a biography / by Martin Gitlin.
       p. cm. — (Greenwood biographies, ISSN 1540–4900)
   Includes bibliographical references and index.
   ISBN 978–0–313–34879–0 (alk. paper)
  1. Diana, Princess of Wales, 1961–1997. 2. Princesses—
Great Britain—Biography.   I. Title.
   DA591.A45D531455   2008
   941.085'092—dc22
   [B]   2008002110

British Library Cataloguing in Publication Data is available.

Library of Congress Catalog Card Number: 2008002110

ISBN: 978–0–313–34879–0
ISSN: 1540–4900

First published in 2008

Greenwood Press, 88 Post Road West, Westport, CT 06881
An imprint of Greenwood Publishing Group, Inc.
www.greenwood.com

Printed in the United States of America

The paper used in this book complies with the
Permanent Paper Standard issued by the National
Information Standards Organization (Z39.48–1984).

10 9 8 7 6 5 4 3 2 1

This book is dedicated to my wife, Mitzi, and our three children, Emily, Melanie, and Andrew, who bring so much joy into my life.

CONTENTS

Photo essay follows page 74

SERIES FOREWORD

In response to high school and public library needs, Greenwood developed this distinguished series of full-length biographies specifically for student use. Prepared by field experts and professionals, these engaging biographies are tailored for high school students who need challenging yet accessible biographies. Ideal for secondary school assignments, the length, format and subject areas are designed to meet educators' requirements and students' interests.

Greenwood offers an extensive selection of biographies spanning all curriculum-related subject areas including social studies, the sciences, literature and the arts, history and politics, as well as popular culture, covering public figures and famous personalities from all time periods and backgrounds, both historic and contemporary, who have made an impact on American and/or world culture. Greenwood biographies were chosen based on comprehensive feedback from librarians and educators. Consideration was given to both curriculum relevance and inherent interest. The result is an intriguing mix of the well known and the unexpected, the saints and sinners from long-ago history and contemporary pop culture. Readers will find a wide array of subject choices from fascinating crime figures like Al Capone to inspiring pioneers like Margaret Mead, from the greatest minds of our time like Stephen Hawking to the most amazing success stories of our day like J.K. Rowling.

While the emphasis is on fact, not glorification, the books are meant to be fun to read. Each volume provides in-depth information about the subject's life from birth through childhood, the teen years, and adulthood.

A thorough account relates family background and education, traces personal and professional influences, and explores struggles, accomplishments, and contributions. A timeline highlights the most significant life events against a historical perspective. Bibliographies supplement the reference value of each volume.

INTRODUCTION

Defining Princess Diana with any sweeping generalizations is an exercise in futility. Those who categorize her solely by her charitable work would be as one-sided in their assessment as others who describe her as a needy soul who searched in vain for true love. Though it remains a pleasant notion to remember Diana for the enormous humanitarian impact she made on the world, it is not realistic to define her solely by those efforts. The princess was an enigmatic figure who led a complex life.

What is certain is that Diana's childhood shaped all that followed. Though her parents loved her, they were often distant and lacking in emotional support. She was mothered and fathered by a series of doting nannies, most of whom she liked, but none who could have possibly replaced a strong emotional bond nurtured by truly committed and adoring parents.

The seeds planted early in life explain Diana's caring side as well. She felt a sense of entitlement for the collection of furry creatures she mothered as a child. At an early age, Diana developed a strong empathy for the weak and less fortunate. Just as she needed someone to take care of her, she understood that those helpless animals required others to look after them, and she did so with every ounce of energy and passion she could muster.

The desire to capture love lost in her formative years and her natural feelings for those in need were the two strongest motivating forces in Diana's life. Though she craved attention and praise, a lack of confidence resulted in poor academic and early job-related performances. She achieved greatness in her role as princess primarily because communicating with people, many of whom were desperately poor and sick, proved a perfect match for her strengths. Indeed, her empathy for others allowed her to become one of the most revered women in history.

Yet her overwhelming desire to find in her personal life the love and affection she received from people throughout the world would haunt her until her tragic death. Though her feelings for Prince Charles began as a teenage crush, there can be little doubt that it blossomed into sincere love by the time they were married in 1981. Though the emotional turmoil raged within both bride and groom, the wedding provided a real-life fairy tale for the world. Millions of viewers throughout the world tuned in, not only to see Diana and Charles enter into a sacred bond, but to watch a nation entranced by the proceedings. The breathtaking beauty of the princess laid a foundation for the adoration she would receive in all her travels.

But sadly, her love for Charles diminished as the years progressed and the realization grew that it would never be returned. His continued affair with Camilla Parker Bowles precluded any possibility of making a commitment to Diana and prevented her from giving all her love to him. As she reached her mid-twenties and matured emotionally and sexually, her emotional attachment to her husband weakened. Aware that he was no longer faithful to her, Diana began searching elsewhere for a fulfilling relationship.

The brilliance and goodness in Princess Diana's adult life materialized in her professional work. Her confidence grew as it became apparent early in her marriage that she was far more popular than her husband, a fact that proved to be a great embarrassment to him. As she reached her late twenties, she displayed a passion and sincerity unmatched by any celebrity of her time. Her eventual separation from Charles allowed her to select the pet charities that tugged most at her heartstrings—invariably those that required the greatest emotional and physical sacrifices.

Others in her position might have chosen to dedicate their time and energy to noncontroversial issues and those that didn't involve the most needy countries or people on the planet. Diana, on the other hand, felt most attracted to those pleading for help. She embraced the homeless, the starving, the children with AIDS, the battered women, and the destitute, and she worked toward the banning of antipersonnel land mines. Her affinity for the care of children didn't require development—it was a natural extension of her childhood. It was Diana taking care of those she deemed to be in need of her love and attention, just as she did with her pets decades earlier.

The power of her persuasion was revealed with every moment, every hug, every glance, from the time an African child asked if she was an angel to the moment she walked bravely through a minefield. Critics argued that it was all a show, but anyone personally touched by the princess vehemently disagreed. And the publicity Diana brought to these issues made a huge difference in the lives of millions. After all, it was only after her visits to those people who had been devastated by antipersonnel land mines in Africa, Asia, and Europe that 122 nations of the world agreed to ban them.

The greatness of a person is judged over time by what that person achieves for those who share the planet. The most hallowed figures in history were beset with personal problems and shortcomings; Diana was no different. But her contributions to the world will long be remembered. The same heart that pined for love so fiercely that it blinded her judgment was also used to give help to the helpless and hope to the hopeless, to feed the hungry, and to provide a ray of sunshine to those who lived in darkness.

Diana remains a beacon for the world, particularly for those who own the resources to better the lives of the hapless millions. Granted, financial contributions are critical to the battles against hunger and homelessness and disease. But the time and inclination to put a famous face on such struggles motivates others to make a difference. Placing the spotlight on a badly needed humanitarian effort is as important as throwing money at it, for it brings awareness. Diana gained a reputation as the people's princess not simply for her relationship with the British people or even with the cheering throngs around the globe. She earned it for the care she gave to those in need, including the forgotten, the downtrodden, the sick, and the starving.

Millions of tears were shed upon Diana's tragic death, as the love she gave the world would be felt no more. Diana can't be judged solely by her selfless, humanitarian acts, but they shall remain her legacy.

TIMELINE: EVENTS IN THE LIFE OF DIANA, PRINCESS OF WALES

1 July 1961	Diana Frances Spencer is born in Norfolk, England.
1967	Summer: Parents Johnnie and Frances separate.
December	Diana is enrolled at Silfield Day School after Johnnie wins custody of her and her brother Charles.
1969	The divorce of parents Johnnie and Frances becomes official.
1970	Diana is sent to Riddlesworth Hall, a prep school in Norfolk.
1973	Diana continues her education at West Heath School in Kent.
1974	Diana moves with her father and siblings to the family estate in Althorp.
14 July 1976	Much to the dismay of Diana and her siblings, Johnnie marries Raine Legge, daughter of romance novelist Barbara Cartland.
1977	Diana leaves West Heath, but Johnnie sends her to a Swiss finishing school, which she attends for only a few months.
	Diana meets Prince Charles through her sister Sarah.
1979	Diana moves to London with three roommates in an apartment bought by her parents. She assumes work as a housekeeper, nanny, and kindergarten teacher's aide.

1980	Charles begins dating Diana.
3 February 1981	The prince asks Diana to marry him during a dinner at Buckingham Palace.
29 July	The wedding of Prince Charles and Diana Spencer is broadcast throughout the world.
5 November	It is officially announced that Diana is pregnant.
21 June 1982	Prince William is born.
March 1983	Diana and Charles tour Australia and New Zealand. Her immense popularity becomes apparent.
15 September 1984	Prince Harry is born.
1988	A conversation with old friend Carolyn Bartholomew convinces Diana to combat her bulimia.
1989	Diana visits Harlem Hospital and Henry Street in New York, showing compassion for the sick, the homeless, and the battered women.
3 June 1991	Prince William is hit in the head with a golf club and suffers a skull fracture. Diana remains by his side while Charles attends a royal engagement, for which he is later criticized.
19 March 1992	Father Johnnie dies of a heart attack.
June	Andrew Morton's biography, *Diana, Her True Story*, is published. Diana's struggles with Charles, bulimia, and depression are revealed.
9 December	Buckingham Palace announces the official separation of Charles and Diana.
1994	An interview with Jonathan Dimbleby reveals that Charles has had a long love affair with Camilla Parker Bowles. He admits to having seen his mistress since 1986.
20 November 1995	A television interview of Diana by journalist Martin Bashir draws an audience of over 20 million viewers.
28 August 1996	Diana and Charles are officially divorced.
January 1997	Diana travels to Africa and launches her campaign against antipersonnel land mines.
July	Tabloid photos surface of Diana on a yacht in the French Riviera with new boyfriend Dodi Al-Fayed.
August	Diana travels to Bosnia to continue her campaign against antipersonnel land mines.

31 August   Diana, Al-Fayed, and driver Henri Paul are killed in a car crash as they speed through a Paris tunnel in an attempt to shed paparazzi.

6 September The funeral of Princess Diana attracts millions. Diana's body is transported from Westminster Abbey and is buried on an island on the Althorp estate.

Chapter 1

BIRTH OF A PRINCESS

Among the millions of little girls of the baby boom generation frolicking about the cities and countryside of England in the mid-1960s, few would have been considered more likely to marry into the royal family than Diana Spencer. But among those born into the British aristocracy, none could have imagined this lonely, thoughtful child becoming a princess and blossoming into one of the most beloved and admired women in history.

It seems only appropriate that a newborn who would bring so much warmth to others would enter the world in early summer. Diana Frances Spencer was born in the late afternoon of July 1, 1961, in her Norfolk, England, home. She was the youngest of three daughters of Edward John Spencer (most commonly referred to as "Johnnie") and first wife Frances. Though Johnnie marveled that the 7-pound, 12-ounce baby was ideal physically, he felt a distinct sense of disappointment that yet another birth had failed to produce a male heir to carry on the Spencer name.

In fact, so hopeful was the couple that Frances would give birth to a boy that they hadn't considered what to name a girl. It wasn't until a week after the birth that they chose Diana Frances, which combined the names of the infant's mother and an eighteenth-century Spencer ancestress who died in her childhood. Johnnie's frustration at the lack of a male child had reached its zenith. He and Frances had already begun raising daughters Elizabeth Sarah and Cynthia Jane when Frances gave birth to a boy. But infant John was so horribly deformed and ill that he survived a mere 10 hours. The baby was taken from Frances upon birth with little explanation. It was the last time she set eyes on her son. For years Frances felt the pain of never having held John. A lung malfunction had taken his life. However, the depression over the death of her baby didn't prevent Frances from immediately trying to become pregnant again. The result was the birth of Diana and heightened disappointment over the lack of a male heir. Yet despite his yearning for a son, Johnnie displayed a particular affection for Diana.

Even at a very young age, Diana sensed problems in the family stemming from the lack of a male child to carry on the Spencer name. Her mother was sent to various London clinics to explore the phenomenon. Young Frances, just 25 years old when she gave birth to Diana, was humiliated and angered by what she deemed to be unfair and pointless examinations. That experience increased Frances's marital discontent, the seeds of which were planted when her newborn son died. Diana never received the opportunity to be raised by parents with a healthy marriage. Diana soon developed a sense of guilt and failure at not being born a boy. As rich as her childhood was materially, it was equally lacking emotionally. Such negative feelings and thoughts damaged her childhood psyche and didn't disappear until she came to grips with them as a young adult. When Frances later gave birth to a son, the arrival of Charles Edward was greeted with far more pomp and circumstance. Diana was christened in a Sandringham church with wealthy commoners named as her godparents. The ceremony for her brother was held at prestigious Westminster Abbey with Queen Elizabeth as principal godparent.

THE HAPPIER SIDE

Despite such obvious differences in treatment and consideration, Diana cherished the joys of her youth. Years after she had gained fame as Princess of Wales, she expressed the pleasures she received from the simplest of sensory experiences. She spoke about the smell of the plastic inside her first stroller, a vivid memory considering how young she had been at the time. Those happy and carefree feelings were few and far between, however. Diana spent her early childhood wondering and often believing she was little more than an annoyance to her family, particularly her parents. She suffered from a belief that if the infant John had survived, she would have never been born. Whether such feelings were justified or self-imposed can only be speculative. Family members often recalled the rejection they perceived Diana to have felt due to the shock over John's death. Second cousin Robert Spencer believed that Diana's self-esteem was quite low as a young child.

A gay and cheerful atmosphere surrounded Diana at Park House, which was nestled near a woodland area just six miles from the Norfolk coast. She was overwhelmed by its enormity, which included playthings for the wealthy such as tennis courts, an outdoor swimming pool, and a cricket pitch. The six-person staff, which included a butler, a cook, and a private governess, were housed in their own private cottages. One activity in which Diana excelled was swimming. Children receive an emotional boost from displaying talent, and she was no different. Adult approval increased her self-esteem, especially in her swimming. Though her father disapproved of her diving off the board at such a young age, she would shout to anyone within earshot so all eyes would be on her as she executed a precise dive into the pool.

Diana was no different from most children in that she was oblivious to much of her surroundings, particularly things that didn't interest her. She spent a great deal of time in a schoolroom in which governess Gertrude Allen taught her and her sisters how to read and write. Diana also enjoyed the company of a ginger-colored cat named Marmalade and the atmosphere in "The Beatle Room," which the children adorned with posters and other memorabilia celebrating the Fab Four, their favorite rock and roll group. Diana's first-floor bedroom was equally captivating. She could gaze out her window at the grazing cattle or creatures such as rabbits and foxes frolicking about on the lawn. Her love for animals seemed boundless. During her childhood, she at various times cared for hamsters, rabbits, guinea pigs, and a goldfish, all of whom she referred to as family members. Upon each pet's demise, she placed it lovingly in a shoebox that she buried in a hole under a spreading cedar tree on the lawn. She even created her own little crosses to mark their graves. Her love for anything furry or feathered would become a trademark of her childhood. That empathetic feeling toward the helpless extended throughout her life. The animals she adored as a youngster were taken care of wonderfully, and she kept the animals and their homes immaculately clean. She understood that they depended on her.

In her more active and carefree moments, Diana and her siblings fed lake trout at nearby Sandringham House, a spot originally built to accommodate guests when Park House was full. She enjoyed walks with her spaniel and swimming in the outdoor pool. By the time she was three years old, she had already become familiar with the joys and challenges of riding horseback. Indeed, few British children could have been doted upon more than Diana, though nanny Judith Parnell gave much of that attention. Diana was far more familiar with Parnell than she was with her own parents. In fact, Diana was nine years old the first time she and her father ate dinner together at the downstairs dining room table. Her parents were kind to her, but she lacked closeness with them. It was a relationship borne out of another era, one of privilege, but lacking in emotion.

Despite the rich surroundings and seemingly endless number of mind-less pursuits, Diana remained troubled. Her self-esteem sunk further as her parents experienced greater marital problems. Various tabloid accounts have strongly suggested and even flatly stated that Johnnie often bullied and sometimes physically struck his wife, which may have contributed to Diana's unhappy and guilt-ridden childhood. The Spencer family has always denied the accusations. Friends and relatives have also expressed their disbelief that violence was ever part of the picture, though they admit Johnnie was certainly plagued by a temper that had developed into a fam-ily trait. He had indeed inherited the rather notable Spencer temper—but violence? Not according to those close to Johnnie. Family members insist that, despite an insensitive side, Johnnie never showed any such signs. Indeed, many believe he preferred to be dominated by Frances.

The age and personality differences between Johnnie and Frances, who was 12 years younger than her husband, became more distinct and de-structive with time. Diana's father liked to remain at home, whereas her mother looked to spread her wings and explore the social opportunities afforded one in the British aristocracy. She traveled often to London for parties. Frances simply got bored staying in Norfolk, partly because of her comparative youth. Her resentment at the treatment she received from her husband and a gnawing, growing feeling that there was more to life than being a wife and mother prompted her to seek fulfillment outside the home. After all, Frances got engaged at the tender age of 17 and wed a year later.

Her discontent and wild side eventually angered Johnnie. During the summer of 1966, about the time Diana was celebrating her fifth birthday, Frances met a young man named Peter Shand Kydd at a dinner party in London. Shand Kydd's family had earned a fortune in the wallpaper business, but he had been more interested in running his sheep ranch in Australia. When that failed, he returned to London. The pair had much in common. Shand Kydd was also married and had three children. Soon there was more than friendship between them. By the time Shand Kydd divorced his wife of 16 years in early 1967, he and Frances were having an affair. The combination of her attraction to Shand Kydd and waning feelings for her husband allowed her to fall in love with her new beau. The marriage of Frances and Johnnie was on borrowed time. In the summer of 1967, the couple decided on a trial separation. Separations and divorces were far less common in the 1960s than they are today, so the announce-ment stunned acquaintances. It also pained the four children.

Though many who blamed Frances for the breakup had accused her of abandoning her children to be with Shand Kydd, she had actually arranged for Charles and Diana to join her in her rented apartment in Belgravia, a district of central London. Charles was enrolled at the nearby kindergarten, and Diana attended classes at the Frances Holland School. Meanwhile, Sarah and Jane were away at their boarding school. Frances wanted to believe the children would remain relatively unaffected by what was intended to be a temporary breakup. Charles and Diana visited their father on weekends, and the entire family would sometimes be together when Johnnie visited them in Belgravia. The family also returned to Park House for short stays, including Christmas. The atmosphere, however, was downright morose when the entire family stayed together. It was apparent the relationship between Johnnie and Frances would never be the same. Even young Diana and Charles could sense that the trial separation was destined to become permanent. They shed many a tear over it, but Frances believed the separation was far preferable to the tension and anger that gripped the home when she and Johnnie were together.

DEATH KNELL OF A MARRIAGE

The final chapter of the breakup was written during the 1967 holiday season. After Frances asked for a divorce, an angry and bitter Johnnie enrolled Diana and Charles at new schools close to his home without informing his wife. Why, he asked, should Frances have the children when she left him? And since the courts were closed at Christmastime, Frances couldn't fight the move. She was forced to return to London without the two children. She attempted to bring back her children after the New Year, but to no avail. She wasn't even allowed inside Park House. Frances recalled one occasion in which she banged on the door and called for the butler to let her in, but she was denied. This was very painful for Frances, as she wanted to let her children know that she hadn't abandoned them, but they couldn't hear her outside their home. Diana, who was then six years old, expressed vivid and painful memories of her mother's stormy departure, which ended all hope of reconciliation. Her feelings weren't soothed in the winter and spring of 1968 as the divorce proceedings increased in bitterness. The children were placed in the middle of a custody battle. Frances had history on her side—the mother generally won custody of the children. She sued for the rights to the kids, but her affair with Shand Kydd worked against her. Even her mother, Ruth, testified against her.

It came as little surprise that the court granted Johnnie custody of the children on the basis of Frances's adultery. But as Frances and Shand Kydd wed on May 2, 1969, and bought a house on the Atlantic coast in West

Sussex, it might not have mattered who received custody. The separation and subsequent divorce of her parents alone would have a profound negative effect on Diana. After all, Diana never truly experienced a healthy family life. She was a mere five years old when the breakup became imminent. Even before that she had never enjoyed consistent, loving contact with either of her parents. She still carried pangs of guilt at being born a girl. And she was far too young to understand the emotional turmoil from which she was suffering. "My parents were busy sorting themselves out," Diana said. "I remember my mother crying, daddy never spoke to us about it. We could never ask questions. Too many nannies. The whole thing was very unstable."[1]

Though Diana couldn't completely hide her unhappiness, she put on quite a strong front. She played unceasingly with her many toys, racing around the driveway on her blue tricycle and taking her many dolls for rides in her stroller. Her instinctive desire to care for others, which defined her adulthood, was already a dominant part of her personality. But the lack of parental love and emotional protection played a role in her fears both before and after the divorce. She and Charles were particularly afraid of the dark. The furry creatures that provided so much fun during the day became rather frightening at night as they noisily went about their business outside Park House. And Johnnie certainly didn't help. On one occasion he informed Diana and Charles that a murderer was loose in the area. They remained awake with eyes wide open, listening fearfully and intently for any sound that might indicate the murderer had broken into their home. After his mother left, Charles sometimes sobbed uncontrollably for her. Diana wanted to be a mother figure for him during those sleepless nights, but her fear of the dark prevented her from leaving her bed to comfort him. She too was overcome by sadness, but she couldn't find the courage to emerge from under her blanket and take care of her brother.

By that time, a revolving door had replaced stability in the employment of nannies to take care of Diana and Charles. Some were rather pleasant, but others proved harsh and unyielding. Johnnie had to fire one nanny who had punished Sarah and Jane by dropping laxatives into their food. Another sadistically banged Diana and Charles on the head with a wooden spoon when they acted up. Though other nannies were kind, they couldn't compare to Frances in the hearts and minds of the children, who considered them all to be unsatisfactory replacements for her. The kids banded together to make life miserable for their nannies, pulling stunts such as locking them in the bathroom and tossing their clothes out the window.

Johnnie's misery didn't make matters any easier. Though he was kind and thoughtful to his children, he immersed himself in his work to keep from drowning in negative thoughts. He remained angry with Frances for her unfaithfulness and prompting the divorce, yet he never criticized her in front of the children. Carefree and happy moments, such as when he brought in a camel for Diana's surprise party on her seventh birthday, were rare during those sad days in the early 1970s. Between work and parenting, Johnnie was simply spread too thin.

The children received little relief from school. As the only students of divorced parents in the building, they felt ostracized. The teachers tried to help, though they were quite affectionate and friendly with all their pupils. The tiny school boasted just 40 students, so all the children received a great deal of individual attention. Toward the end of Diana's enrollment there, one teacher drew a troubling conclusion about Diana's mind-set. She wrote of what she perceived as Diana's defeatist attitude and a troubling future if that weakness wasn't overcome. Diana was far from outgoing with her classmates, both inside and outside the classroom. Her muddled mind during that period of her life also affected her studies. She sometimes became so emotionally pained that she burst into tears during class, which alarmed the teacher and students. Sadly, her artwork was always dedicated to her divorced parents.

It was at this point that Diana developed what has been described as a jealousy toward Charles, who had earned the praise of his teachers for his studious nature, behavior, and performance in the classroom. She yearned for positive attention. It wasn't always enough for her to feel good about what she did well, such as swimming and dancing. She felt a need for others to notice and express their appreciation. But despite the strain in her relationship with Charles, she felt closer to him than she did her two older sisters, largely because they spent most of their time away at boarding school. And since Diana had strong maternal instincts, even as a small child, she was protective of her little brother. His suffering was her suffering after the divorce. Diana also tended to stretch the truth quite often. The problem intensified after the breakup of her parents. In one instance, a school official who was driving Diana home told her that she would force her out of the car if she told one more fib.

The home she referred to was Park House, but Diana and Charles didn't really have one home. They stayed with their mother in London every weekend and for two weeks during the Christmas holidays. Throughout those periods, Frances shed many tears over the limited time the court deemed she could spend with them. She missed Diana and Charles even when they were in her company. Frances cried over the prospect of her kids leaving when the weekend was over. Her children were equally pained over bouncing from one home to the other during the holidays. They received plenty of presents, but not enough time to be loved and cherished by either parent.

BREAK FROM HOME

Diana received a badly needed retreat from Park House in 1970, when she was enrolled at Riddlesworth Hall, a boarding school in Norfolk located two hours away. A sense of rejection by her father caused her to balk at first, but she quickly warmed up to the idea. Riddlesworth provided an academic and social outlet for Diana. Not only was she taught English, math, history, and science, but she also received firsthand experience in living and getting along with others. As do many boarding schools, Riddlesworth emphasized social skills such as proper manners. Though Diana expanded her horizons at Riddlesworth, she was allowed to care for her beloved animals and those of her classmates as head of the Pets' Corner. Among the pets was Peanuts, who won first prize for "Best Kept Guinea Pig."

Despite her growth athletically—she continued to excel in swimming and diving—Diana proved quite ordinary academically. She simply blended in with the other students, but the staff did take notice of Johnnie when he dropped off and picked up his daughter. His outgoing and amiable personality was memorable. Headmaster Patricia Wood and her staff admit that they remember Johnnie with far more clarity than they do Diana, who simply blended in with the other girls at Riddlesworth.

Diana would inherit the genuine interest and concern her father had for others. Though it would be many years before she was confident enough in herself to blossom socially, such traits would eventually make her one of the most adored figures of the twentieth century. How did Diana's rich family history play a role in her upbringing and adult life? An examination of her roots explains a great deal.

NOTE

1. Andrew Morton, *Diana: Her True Story* (New York: Simon and Schuster, 1997), 18.

Chapter 2

A FAMILY HISTORY

During the more turbulent moments of her life, Diana often repeated the following to herself: "Remember you're a Spencer."[1] She spoke those words with a distinct sense of pride. They reminded her to toughen herself in difficult emotional times. After all, the Spencers had enjoyed centuries of wealth, achievement, and notoriety in Britain.

Family success could be traced back to what became known as the Glorious Revolution of 1688, in which the Whigs helped overthrow King Charles II. The throne was handed to George I, placing the Whig theorists in power until the early nineteenth century. Though party politics had yet to form in Britain until after the American Revolution, the Whigs had been established as a group fighting against absolute rule and siding with the great aristocratic families of Britain. The Spencers of those generations supported the Whig populist beliefs. They had already gained vast wealth through sheep farming, then wool trading. By the 1400s, the family owned huge tracts of land in Warwickshire, Northamptonshire, Buckinghamshire, and Hertfordshire. John Spencer built a family center home at Althorp in 1508. The 121-room mansion sat on a sprawling 13,000 acres. The Whigs were the "most serious, exclusive and illustrious cousinhood, held together by birth, blood and breeding," wrote historian David Cannadine. "They were the embodiment of glamour and grandeur, high rank and high living."[2]

During the next two centuries, the Spencers spread out into what is now Greater London. They owned land in Claphan, Wandsworth, and Wimbledon. Though they were related to the royal families of Charles II and James II, the aristocratic Spencers considered themselves to be of higher class. The Spencers didn't sit on their wealth. They purchased high-society items such as rare books and artwork and placed them throughout Althorp House. Johnnie's father, Jack, the 7th Earl Spencer, was particularly proud and protective of the valuable collection. Jack's son, however, felt downright claustrophobic remaining indoors, safeguarding the treasures. At a young age, he reveled in outdoor activities. Such differences in personalities and priorities strained the relationship between Jack and Johnnie. Jack's legendary temper certainly didn't ease tensions.

The argument that opposites attract certainly received a boost from Jack and his wife, Cynthia, who was the daughter of the Duke of Abercorn. While Jack was a picture of aristocratic snobbery, Cynthia was sensitive and kind to those in all stations of life. Such qualities as empathy and compassion for others were eventually passed on to Diana. The Spencer family never achieved nor rarely strived for power, but their wealth and breeding certainly made them well known in the political world. The Spencers at various points in history served as Knights of the Garter, First Lord of the Admiralty, and ambassadors. Among their kin were seven American presidents and famed actor Humphrey Bogart.

Frances's ancestors were no less influential. Early on the Fermoys made their mark in Ireland. Diana's great-great-grandfather Edmund Burke Roche was voted into the Irish Parliament and later became a baron. Son James Roche wed an American named Frances (Fanny) Work, whose father, Frank, was a wealthy stockbroker who brought tremendous sums of money into the family. The marriage failed, however, and Frank threatened to withhold the infusion of such riches into the family if grandsons Maurice and Francis were not educated in America. The grandsons fulfilled their grandfather's wish, which prompted Frank to leave Maurice and Francis $2.9 million apiece upon his death in 1911. The two men took their money back to England in 1921. Maurice fell in love with a beautiful Scottish pianist named Ruth Gill, who was only half his age and was to become Diana's grandmother. Maurice had become close to British royalty. He forged a friendship with the Duke of York, who later became King George VI. Ruth and Queen Elizabeth also developed a close bond, as they shared a love of music. The Fermoys were responsible for the purchase of Park House in Norfolk. King George V handed the lease over to Diana's grandfather Maurice, otherwise known as the 4th Baron Fermoy, who eventually landed in the British Parliament.

ANOTHER GENERATION

Frances was born in 1936, the second of three children born to Maurice and Ruth. She was raised aristocratically to the core, surrounded by nannies and governesses. She learned proper etiquette in all areas of personal and social life, and she both respected and adored her parents. She considered her father compassionate and sensitive and spoke glowingly about her mother's confidence and drive. But whether or not it was related to their parents' upbringing, the Roche siblings lived in turmoil. Frances's sister Mary suffered through three divorces and lived in seclusion in London after Ruth passed away. Brother Edmund, the 5th Baron Fermoy, battled depression and committed suicide in 1984 at the age of 45. Frances showed great intelligence and a love for the arts during her youth, but she was far from snobbish or dull. Rather, she boasted a fine sense of humor. She had a dominant personality, one that attracted Johnnie to her.

That relationship began after her coming-out ball in London several months after her 17th birthday in April 1953. In addition to being 12 years older than Frances, Johnnie was already engaged, to Lady Anne Coke, who was the eldest daughter of the Earl and Countess of Leicester and the same age as Frances. Johnnie was overwhelmed by Frances's beauty. He quickly broke his engagement and began courting Frances. The couple became engaged when Johnnie asked for her hand in marriage during a break from playing tennis at Park House. Frances disregarded the age difference with the knowledge that for several generations the Fermoy women tended to marry much older men. The engagement remained firm despite a previous commitment that sent Johnnie to Australia for six months. The couple married in June 1954 at Westminster Abbey. The gathering of more than 1,000 guests included Queen Elizabeth and Prince Philip among those representing the royal family.

After honeymooning throughout Europe, Johnnie and Frances settled in a house on the grounds of Althorp, but their clash of personalities became magnified by their polar opposite feelings for those hallowed halls. Frances considered the home quite dreary. She believed the collections of valuable artwork and porcelain gave their residence the feel of a museum rather than a cozy home. Though Frances professed her happiness during the early years of their marriage and immediately set out to have children ("honeymoon baby" Sarah was born nine months after the wedding), she was turned off by the constant bickering between Jack and Johnnie. She also began feeling twinges of restlessness that would eventually lead to the demise of the marriage. Her sense of independence didn't go over well with the conservative Spencer clan. Johnnie, however, was amenable to the wishes of his new wife. After Maurice passed away in 1955, she and Johnnie took up residence at Park House. Frances inherited more than $300,000, allowing the couple to purchase 236 acres of additional land, doubling their previous acreage. Johnnie farmed the land and increased his involvement with various charities, particularly the National Association of Boys' Clubs.

The first years at Park House were blissful. The couple traveled often and cultivated relationships with their aristocratic friends. Frances enjoyed starting a family, but the death of baby John changed everything. It cast a pall over the marriage that was never lifted. During the early period of the disintegration of her parents' marriage, Diana was far too young to understand its reasons, though she instinctively knew there was a problem. Even as a toddler she was already displaying the personality traits inherited from her ancestors. Like grandmother Cynthia, she genuinely cared for those less fortunate. Like Johnnie, she showed an innate ability to communicate with others. And like Frances, her strong will was quite distinctive at an early age.

Also like Frances, she abhorred her occasional visits to the Althorp home, which simply frightened her. As one might expect from a young child, she did not appreciate its history. Other children might have found the spooky hallways and the portraits of dead ancestors intriguing, but not Diana—and not her brother. Charles recalled Althorp as impersonal and overwhelming, like a club for a bygone era with the ticking of clocks irritating its visitors. He considered it particularly uninviting and even downright scary for children. It's no wonder he balked when told he was heading there as a youngster. They had no choice in 1975, when Johnnie moved the family to Althorp after Jack died unexpectedly from pneumonia.

Diana was now a teenager, and her strengths and weaknesses had become more pronounced. Though sister Jane was by far the strongest student in the family, Diana fawned over the rebellious Sarah, for whom she ran errands endlessly. But then, Diana rarely balked at performing her own chores or aiding others. She earned the Legett Cup for helpfulness at Riddlesworth, an honor that pleased grandmother Cynthia, the Countess Spencer, whose feelings of kinship for Diana were quite mutual. When Cynthia died from a brain tumor in 1972, it came as quite a shock to the sensitive child. The heartbroken Diana believed that her grandmother still protected her spiritually.

IN HER SISTERS' FOOTSTEPS

Diana soon followed Sarah and Jane to the West Heath boarding school in Kent. Like Riddlesworth, West Heath attempted to infuse its students with confidence and a strong character; its emphasis was only partly academic. But which sister would Diana follow? Would she emulate eldest sister Sarah, who despite her involvement in theater and swimming, was expelled at one point for her lack of discipline? Or would she follow the lead of Jane, a well-behaved and brilliant student who followed a straight and narrow path? Even Charles had developed into an academic standout at Maidwell Hall in Northamptonshire, a prelude to his college career at prestigious Oxford.

Diana seemed to choose the former early in her career at West Heath. Indeed, she reveled in breaking away from the tedium of life at West Heath. She accepted one dare to walk a half mile down the driveway in the middle of the night to secure some sweets from a woman named Polly Phillimore. She performed her task, only to discover there was nobody there. She returned down the long driveway with police cars entering the scene and noticed all the lights in the school had been turned on. She discovered later that the police presence was due to one of her roommates complaining of appendicitis and not due to her absence. The stunt nearly cost her enrollment at the boarding school, but Diana simply figured that life was rather boring, so why not take a dare? Her divorced parents were called into the school, but neither was angry with Diana. In fact, her father expressed joy that his heretofore-shy daughter had shown such pluck. Diana continued to accept dares, including eating huge amounts of food in one sitting, never mind that it sometimes landed her in the company of the school nurse. West Heath principal Ruth Rudge, who claimed not to have recalled the incident, remembered Diana as suspicious of adults and often mildly unfriendly to her classmates. Rudge added that Diana blossomed when she grew to know and understand those with whom she associated. She believed that adults needed to earn her trust before she opened up to them.

Longtime friend Carolyn Pride (later Carolyn Bartholomew), who occupied the bed next to Diana in their dormitory and later shared her London flat, recalled a distinct difference between the behavior of Diana and that of Jane. Diana and Carolyn shared the unenviable distinction of being two of the few pupils at West Heath whose parents were divorced. Carolyn considered Jane popular and sweet but rather plain, and she thought of Diana as far more lively. Diana struggled academically at West Heath. Though she took more interest in subjects involving people, such as history, and enjoyed writing, she performed poorly on tests. Grades of "D," which constituted failing at West Heath, were commonplace.

But while she failed to match the success of her siblings in the classroom, another side of Diana continued to develop. She began to act on her desire to care for others. Whereas she felt sympathy for her animals as a small child, she now showed empathy for seniors, as well as the physically and mentally ill. Among the hospitals Diana visited during that time was Darenth Park, which housed the physically and mentally handicapped. It was an imposing place for the students at West Heath, who had little experience interacting with these individuals. Trip organizer Muriel Stevens marveled at how well Diana handled the situation. Most of the handicapped people were in wheelchairs, and others had to be encouraged to leave their seats to greet the visitors. Many patients rushed up to them or grabbed at them, which frightened many of the students. Diana, however, only felt more empathy toward the patients. Stevens saw her as relaxed and in her element, which she considered remarkable.

Diana and a classmate took weekly trips to one particular senior in Sevenoaks. They enjoyed tea, biscuits, and conversation with her, and then helped her with her shopping. During that same period, she visited an area mental hospital, where she entertained the patients by dancing with them. She not only did volunteer work, but she discovered that she genuinely cared for those less fortunate and that she was blessed with talent in that area. Those with whom she worked appreciated her and enjoyed her personality. They sensed that Diana genuinely cared about them. As they would with many youngsters, such accomplishments raised her feeling of self-worth.

So did her talents in athletics and the arts. Diana not only excelled as a swimmer and diver, winning several events, but she also played a strong game of tennis. She studied piano and won her school dance competition in 1976. Diana enjoyed participating in sports and in the arts, but she preferred to excel in activities in which her sisters and ancestors hadn't already established themselves. Grandmother Cynthia and sister Sarah were noted for their excellence as pianists. Her mother and sisters were accomplished athletes. Diana resented family involvement in her participation both in sports and in the arts. Such could not be claimed in regard to her community work, which strengthened her self-image because nobody else played a role in her achievements. Upon the family's move to Althorp, she practiced her ballet only when she had made certain no family or friends were watching. Among Diana's favorite activities was tap dancing, but she enjoyed a myriad of sports and dance forms. She refuted those who claimed she disregarded certain school subjects. Though she didn't excel in some of them, she spoke later in life about her love for the piano and interest in tap dancing, as well as sports such as tennis, netball, and hockey.

"RAINE, RAINE, GO AWAY"

Diana soon had another important adult in her life: the Countess of Dartmouth Raine Legge, with whom Johnnie began forging a personal relationship. The couple met in 1972, when the family still lived at Park House. The beautiful countess with a sharp intellect and a driven personality was married with four children, but she fell in love with Johnnie. The four Spencer children conspired to make her first date with their father quite unpleasant. They considered Johnnie to be theirs alone, and all others who wished to enter his personal life were seen as intruders. When Lady Dartmouth arrived at Park House for lunch and the girls treated her coldly, she didn't acknowledge their unfriendliness. Rather, she remained gracious. Sarah decided to take the rudeness a step further. She belched loudly and deliberately and was sharply reprimanded by her father. Sarah replied sarcastically that belching is considered an expression of appreciation in Arab countries, whereupon her father ordered her from the table.

Diana quickly sided with Sarah. When admonished by Johnnie to keep quiet, she claimed she didn't feel well and asked to be excused. Her embarrassed father quickly sent her away as well.

The children's dislike of Raine, particularly considering it was their initial meeting, might be classified as pure jealousy. But Charles recalled their objections to her as going beyond that, though they couldn't be easily placed. He and his siblings felt an immediate and instinctive dislike and distrust for her. Lady Dartmouth wasn't deterred in the least. A determined woman both personally and professionally, she was quite well known as the daughter of Barbara Cartland, Diana's favorite novelist. She had forged her own reputation as a strong-opinioned woman on various councils. She furthered her career as chairman of the Historic Buildings Board and member of the English Tourist Board. Lady Dartmouth was also politically active. When she resigned from a government advisory committee on the environment, she was lauded by some and criticized by others. Her name became even more recognized throughout the country for her attractive features, stylish dress, and ability to gain positions of power. A professional relationship strengthened the bond between Raine and Johnnie, who preferred women with strong personalities. As chairman of the United Kingdom Executive Committee for European Architectural Heritage in 1975, which was dedicated to preserving historic towns and buildings, she authored a book titled *What Is Our Heritage?* She asked Johnnie to help the cause through his chairmanship of the National Association of Boys' Clubs.

The mutual attraction between Johnnie and Raine was obvious. To Diana, who enjoyed taking care of her father and considered herself the apple of his eye, Raine was a threat. Coupled with the move to Althorp, Raine's increased presence in her life both saddened and angered Diana. She not only lost her Norfolk friends, but she gained an unwelcome future stepmother. She recalled Raine showering her and her siblings with gifts, but she also feared that Raine would take their father away from them.

Diana's other loss was the warmth of Park House and the surrounding neighborhood. Though set in the beautiful rolling hills of the English countryside, the Althorp mansion itself gave off a stately, cold, impersonal feel. Diana, however, learned to appreciate the storied history of Althorp and kept herself busy doing household chores and even preparing her specialty, bread and butter pudding, for the servants. She and her siblings had stripped themselves of the fear of Althorp they felt as little children and began to enjoy its treasures, such as the front staircase they gleefully slid down on a tea tray.

Shortly thereafter, Raine moved in, and any joy for the children disappeared. She had yet to marry Johnnie, but she was invited to occupy a room close to that of her future husband. The kids didn't care that she had a tremendous sum of money, some of which she used to redecorate Althorp. She began to fear that the resentment she felt from the Spencer children would spoil her plans to wed Johnnie. Sarah, being the eldest and perhaps the most hostile toward Raine, took the lead in attempting to dissuade her. She even used the media to bad-mouth her father's girlfriend in an attempt to poison the relationship. Diana and her siblings sometimes even chanted, "Raine, Raine, go away" within earshot of Lady Dartmouth. But she wasn't going anywhere, not with her sights set on Johnnie. Husband Gerald Dartmouth was granted a divorce on the grounds of adultery in May 1976, which freed her to marry Johnnie two months later in London. He didn't want to incur his children's wrath before the wedding, so he didn't tell them until afterward. The delay only heightened their anger. Sarah, who found out not through her father but through a newspaper article, informed Diana that they had a new, unwanted stepmother. Diana confronted Johnnie, which led to a rather violent encounter:

> [Johnnie] said, "I want to explain to you why, um, I've got married to Raine." And I said, "Well, we don't like her." And he said, "I know that, but you'll grow to love her, as I have." And I said, "Well, we won't." I kept on saying we, not I. I was the little crusader here . . . and I got really angry and I, if I remember rightly, I slapped him across the face, and I said, "That's from all of us, for hurting us" and walked out of the room and slammed the door. He followed me and he got me by the wrist and turned me round and said, "Don't you ever talk to me like that again." And I said, "Well, don't you ever do that to us again," and walked off.[3]

Though Diana never developed a fondness for Althorp, she resented Raine for selling various bits of the vast collection stored in the stately home to pay inheritance taxes and fund the renovations she desired. Diana felt that the historical greatness and whatever homey atmosphere Althorp did have when they moved in was eliminated by the bright, shiny look orchestrated by the new Countess Spencer.

While Diana was resentful and angry at the permanent addition of Raine into the family, Sarah was affected even more profoundly. She had fallen in love with Gerald Grosvenor, the Duke of Westminster. The consensus among family and friends was that the relationship was destined to end in marriage, but it ended rather abruptly. The emotionally shattered young woman soon developed an eating disorder that was attributed to the breakup. The once beautiful and vibrant oldest Spencer sibling wasted away, dropping to an emaciated 77 pounds. Sarah was stricken with both anorexia and bulimia. She at times starved herself, but sometimes ate in excess before self-induced vomiting. Such diseases weren't recognized as particularly widespread until at least a decade later, but Sarah recalled that she looked emaciated. She was forced to shop in the children's clothing department, but she refused to admit she had a problem. Even as thin as she was, she convinced herself she looked beautiful. Diana was greatly concerned. When she visited Sarah at her apartment during time away from West Heath, her sister attempted to hide the eating disorder. But it was hard for Diana not to notice the 35-pound weight loss in her already-slim sister.

NOTES

1. Sally Bedell Smith, *Diana in Search of Herself* (New York: Times Books, 1999), 20.

2. Ibid.

3. Sarah Bradford, *Diana* (New York: Viking Press, 2006), 34.

Chapter 3

DIANA THE TEENAGER

Little did Diana know that she would eventually become a victim of the same eating disorders that Sarah suffered from, though there had been indications of obsessive behavior, particularly when it came to food. After all, the young girl joyfully took dares at school to wolf down three kippers and six pieces of bread. Whether she was purging at that time is speculative.

The psychiatric community had identified anorexia by that time, but bulimia was another matter. The study of various eating disorders wouldn't intensify until the following decades. Those close to Diana at West Heath spoke often of her prodigious eating habits. Even she admitted to a significant appetite. She would gorge on midnight snacks, secretly bringing food into her room against the rules. Yet the amount of food she consumed didn't result in a weight gain.

Such obsessive behavior had been a part of Diana's life for years. Even at age six, when the bedrooms of most children look like they have been struck by a tornado, Diana kept hers excessively neat. She even cleaned up after her classmates during her early school years. It has been offered that Diana's obsessive desire to remain in control of her weight and her surroundings was in response to her overwhelming feelings of stress as a child. Child and adolescent psychiatrist and psychoanalyst Dr. Kent Ravenscroft offered that Diana's neatness was an extension of her desire to clean up her bad feelings.[1] He claimed that her urges toward messiness were overcome by a need to keep things in order and manage her life.

So were binging and purging. Diana's own eating disorders as a teenager weren't heavily publicized until she spoke frankly about them shortly before her death in 1997. Previous to that time, she blamed the cold treatment she received from Prince Charles during their engagement for the problem. She later admitted that bulimia had taken hold a few years earlier. She told patients at Roehampton Priory, a private clinic outside London, that she blamed her idolizing of Sarah for her own eating disorder.

The girl who would eventually blossom into a beautiful princess and the most photographed woman in the world didn't turn heads. Nor did she strike strangers as having the grace and charm of royalty. Diana, who was pleasant-looking throughout her life, appeared rather gangly and awkward as a young teenager. Such lack of assuredness is common at that age, but those in aristocratic families are judged differently. Among those who expressed a rather negative first impression of Diana was Lucinda Craig Harvey, a London housemate of Sarah's who met Diana during a cricket match at Althorp. Harvey spoke unflatteringly about what she considered Diana's frumpy dresses and overall shyness and unsophisticated air.

The trauma of her father's marriage to Raine played a role in Diana's mind-set during that period of her life. She was highly sensitive, and she perceived herself as unintelligent, particularly in comparison to her siblings. Her jealousy of Charles was heightened during her later years at West Heath. Her failure in two critical sets of exams that would have resulted in her promotion forced her to leave school at age 16. Several factors have been attributed to Diana's lack of progress academically. She still suffered from feelings that her parents gave birth to her merely to replace baby John, who didn't survive his first day. She felt a sense of guilt for not being born a boy. That she felt betrayed by her father, whom she considered lost to Raine, is undeniable. Classmates and friends, however, have claimed that Diana's poor performance in school was merely a result of her laziness during that period of her life.

DIANA'S SENSE OF DESTINY

Some individuals believed that a strong sense of her ultimate place in the world guided Diana. Biographer Sarah Bradford perceived that Diana developed an inner belief in herself and her instincts that guided her throughout her life. She added that Diana believed there was a higher calling that separated her from others.[2] If that was the case, schoolwork might not have seemed particularly important, yet Diana was devastated by her failure in the classroom. It seemed to cement the perception of her that she believed her family held. She spoke of a feeling of hopelessness and despair, which translated into a jealousy of Charles, who performed quite well academically. She was hurt by her belief that her family considered her unintelligent. Diana recalled weeping in the company of the headmistress over her failures.

At a time when Diana needed reassurance from her father, Raine was receiving all of Johnnie's attention. Rather than foster a healthy inclusive relationship with all the family members, she battled against the children for Johnnie's time. And since he was attracted to dominant women, he didn't mind. He always felt and showed love toward his kids, but many close to the family believe he allowed Raine to manipulate the situation to her benefit. A social butterfly with dozens of wealthy and influential acquaintances, Raine often arranged parties at Althorp during which the kids were sent elsewhere. The children were away at boarding school much of that time, so Raine didn't always need to act on her possessiveness. She had Johnnie all to herself.

Though Diana struggled at school, her frustration was turned inward. She rarely displayed anger or bitterness to those close to her. The Althorp staff grew particularly fond of her. One couple who enjoyed her company was butler Ainslie Pendrey and his housekeeper wife, Maud, who were attracted to Diana's shyness during the girl's visits every six or seven weeks. Ainslie would make certain all her favorite foods were available in the kitchen whenever Diana was home. They appreciated her politeness and didn't mind spoiling her. Diana eventually opened up to the couple, which they also enjoyed. They spoke later about how the entire staff enjoyed her sweet nature and that Diana would invariably find a bouquet of flowers on her bed when she arrived at Althorp. Ainsley predicted that Diana would be something quite special someday.

It wouldn't take very long, but Diana had to slip away from her academic life before she would indeed blossom. She followed Sarah to the Institut Alpin Vidamanette, a finishing school in Switzerland for the well-to-do that enrolled mostly Spanish and Italian girls but enforced a rule that students must speak French. Not only did Diana continue to speak English, but she also became bored with her class work in the stereotypically female domestic science training. Moreover, she simply didn't want to attend school anymore. All she enjoyed in Switzerland was skiing. She wrote letter after letter to her parents, sometimes up to four a day, begging them to let her come home. She argued that they were wasting their money and her time by keeping her at a school hundreds of miles from her home with which she felt nothing but disdain. She eventually convinced them to allow her to return home.

In September 1978, another chapter was written in Diana's relationship with her father and stepmother, one that cemented her feelings for both. During a visit with friends in Norfolk, she felt a strong premonition that Johnnie was going to take ill and perhaps even die. Incredibly and terribly, Johnnie indeed collapsed from a massive cerebral hemorrhage the following day as he strolled across the Althorp courtyard. He was transported unconscious to Northampton General Hospital. The facility wasn't reputable enough for Raine, who insisted that her husband be taken to the National Hospital for Nervous Diseases in London. At just 54 years old, Johnnie had fallen into a coma and was placed on life support. Raine remained by his side in a desperate hope for his survival. Surgeons worked feverishly on his brain for four hours. Johnnie appeared to have recovered, but less than a month later he was transferred to Brompton Hospital after having contracted a rare bacterium that proved untreatable by typical antibiotics.

He was nearly pronounced dead on several occasions, but Raine refused to give up hope. She contacted acquaintance Bill Cavendish-Bentnick, the director of German pharmaceutical giant Bayer, who later became Duke of Portland, in what appeared to be a vain attempt to find a new drug that could save her husband's life. Indeed, there was one—a test product called Azlocillin. The use of such a drug not yet on the market would require approval from Johnnie's doctors, who eventually relented. Fantastically, it worked. Raine had saved his life.

Such dedication to their father failed to spur a healthier and friendlier relationship between Raine and the children. Instead, they visited their father only when Raine was gone. When they did meet, the children expressed nothing but derision. Diana believed that Raine prevented her and her siblings from seeing their father, which prompted Sarah to take the lead in trying to get them into the hospital, generally to no avail. They feared that their father simply believed his offspring didn't want to see him. The episode further heightened tensions between Raine and the children. But their stepmother, as usual, was unflappable. She again took a "me against them" approach. While Diana and her siblings were complaining that nurses were told to keep them away from their critically ill father, Raine indicated that it was the children who attempted to keep her out. "I'm a survivor and people forget that at their peril," she said years later. "There's pure steel up my backbone. Nobody destroys me, and nobody was going to destroy Johnnie so long as I could set by his bed—some of his family tried to stop me—and will my life force into him."[3]

FATEFUL ENCOUNTER

Later, another man entered Diana's life, but he entered it through her eldest sister. Prince Charles met 22-year-old Sarah at a house party at

Windsor Castle. Charles showed an immediate interest despite noticing that Sarah was painfully thin. He even inquired as to whether she was anorexic. The disease was so pronounced at first that Frances had taken Sarah to the hospital. The immediate attraction between Charles and Sarah seemed greatly based on their personalities. The prince had become bored with what he perceived as the haughty, often dull group of people in his circle of acquaintances, so he deemed Sarah's rebellious nature and irreverent sense of humor to be quite refreshing. It didn't take long for the British media to pick up on the affairs of the young couple. Photos of Sarah accompanying the prince to various events began to appear in the tabloids. But Charles was apparently less impressed by Sarah's physical appearance than by her other attributes. Sarah was taken aback that Charles hadn't attempted to promote a sexual encounter.

Diana's life changed dramatically in November 1977, when she took the weekend off late in her enrollment at West Heath to visit Sarah at Althorp and meet her new beau. Charles and Diana set eyes upon each other for the first time in a plowed field near Nobottle Wood. Sarah indignantly expressed the feeling that her sister unabashedly flirted with the prince. That Sarah felt threatened was not surprising. Diana had begun to blossom as she reached age 16, and she became more cheerful. The sense of humor she had always possessed turned outward as she stripped herself of the shyness that gripped her as a child. Diana gained confidence as her feelings of inadequacy lessened. She was no longer the girl who felt unwanted because her parents yearned for a boy at her birth. Time had healed that wound. Her innate social skills and genuine interest in others had always attracted others to her—added to her newfound confidence, she had become the life of any party.

Diana was indeed flattered at the dance that evening at Althorp when it became apparent that Charles wished to spend time with her. She was thrilled that she didn't need to put on airs for the prince to show an interest in her. Sarah felt quite the opposite. Diana recalled Charles asking her that evening if he could see the prestigious Althorp picture gallery. Diana quickly agreed, but Sarah pushed her aside and took over. Diana felt both thrilled and surprised that the prince showed an interest in her. She knew instinctively that he was taken with her.

Diana's early relationship with the prince was far from one-sided. Though later in life she spoke often about Charles's pursuit of her, others have spoken about the infatuation she felt toward him. It's certainly understandable that a heretofore shy, unconfident young woman would feel smitten by a dashing young prince who showed an interest in her. West Heath piano instructor Penny Walker, who gave Diana lessons, recalled that her pupil was indeed taken by the prince. Walker remembered her speaking in glow-ing terms about having met and spent time with Charles. In fact, she rec-ollected Diana talking of little else and remarking enthusiastically on the subject. Walker saw nothing unusual about it, particularly since Diana was a teenager who would naturally be excited by such an encounter. Receiv-ing interest from a prince is, after all, something that belongs in a fairy tale, even for one raised in an aristocratic background, such as Diana.

A marriage was also about to change the life of Jane, who was 20 when she wed childhood friend Robert Fellowes, a 36-year-old Royal Scots Guardsman whom she knew growing up in Norfolk. The ceremony was held at the Guards Chapel in the Wellington Barracks, a stone's throw away from famed Buckingham Palace. Frances sprung for the entire wedding, but she played second fiddle to Raine, who busily tended to organizing the event. The tension between Frances and Johnnie was evident throughout the wedding, which was attended by members of the royal family.

It wouldn't be the only tension involving a member of the Spencer family. Sarah's careless promotion of a dialogue with the British tabloid press angered Prince Charles and led to the demise of their relationship. When Sarah accompanied the prince to a skiing party in Switzerland in February 1978, the tabloids featured photos of the couple on the slopes. Prince Charles, it was written, had a new girlfriend. Sarah enjoyed the at-tention and granted a long interview with *Woman's Own* magazine about her relationship with the prince and much more. She spoke about a drink-ing problem that resulted in her expulsion from school. She spoke about her anorexia, fibbing that a gynecologist had informed her that she could never have children (she eventually gave birth to three). She spoke about having countless boyfriends.

Then she rambled on about Prince Charles, speaking about his roman-tic tendencies and his penchant for falling in love easily. She added that she was not in love with him, because she was not one to be taken in by slow courtships. She went on to say that she would already be engaged to Charles if the two were meant to be together, and that if he did ask her, she would turn him down because neither of them was ready to be married. She concluded that she enjoyed more of a brotherly-sisterly re-lationship with the prince. Though nothing Sarah mentioned about her relationship with Charles stretched the truth, the prince was livid that she spoke to tabloid reporters about her feelings for him and those she perceived he had about her.

While Sarah was falling out of favor with Charles, her parents didn't know what to do with Diana. Diana had yet to turn 17 when she returned from England after leaving the finishing school in Switzerland. Her disdain for Raine drove her back to Frances. She moved in with two friends at her mother's home in Chelsea, even through Frances was living in Scotland. She enjoyed the same financial support from her parents that she had as a child. Johnnie and Frances strongly urged her to prepare for her future, but Diana simply didn't boast the skills or experience to land a job suited for a young adult. She worked briefly as a nanny, then took three-month courses in both cooking and teaching ballet, the second resulting in a position at a ballet studio teaching two-year-olds.

What appeared to be a perfect first real job for Diana was anything but. Though she always enjoyed dancing and working with young children, she simply wasn't ready for a daily work routine away from family and friends. The pressure of teaching toddlers to dance while their mothers and nannies looked on overwhelmed Diana. After three months, she suddenly quit. Stress wasn't the only reason Diana left that job prematurely. She had also torn all the tendons in her left ankle during a ski trip in the French Alps with friend Mary-Ann Stewart-Richardson.

Though the tumble down the slopes had a negative effect on Diana professionally, the excursion proved quite eventful. Diana not only considered it one of the most enjoyable holidays of her young life, but she established new friendships that would remain with her through much of her adult life. These budding relationships were not with anyone in the Stewart-Richardson family, who were using the ski trip as an escape from the morose reminders of a recent family tragedy. Diana felt uncomfortable staying in their chalet while they grieved, so she quickly accepted when Simon Berry, whose father had made a fortune in the wine business, asked her to join his group instead. Berry and his friends were young and ambitious, having founded their own travel agency. Diana thoroughly enjoyed their company, joining them in singing silly songs and partaking in pillow fights. Her new friends ridiculed her good-naturedly when she spoke about a framed picture of Prince Charles taken in 1969 she had displayed prominently in her dorm room. She claimed the school gave it to her.

There would be far more serious talk about Diana and Prince Charles in the years to come. But first, she needed to get her personal and professional lives in order, and that would require some help from her family.

NOTES

1. Sally Bedell Smith, *Diana in Search of Herself* (New York: Times Books, 1999), 61.

2. Sarah Bradford, *Diana* (New York: Viking Press, 2006), 47.

3. Andrew Morton, *Diana: Her True Story* (New York: Simon and Schuster, 1997), 39.

Chapter 4

MERGING PATHS

As Diana approached her 18th birthday, she emerged from her shell socially. Though she had matured to a great extent, she still lacked confidence. The depressing days in which she felt guilty about being born a girl were gone, but she still carried with her a poor self-image. The turmoil caused by her parents' divorce, her comparatively poor academic performance, and her early failures professionally still weighed heavily on her.

Among those who befriended Diana on the ski vacation to the French Alps was Adam Russell, a deer farmer whose direct ancestry included former British prime minister Stanley Baldwin. Diana got to know Russell particularly well because he too was confined to the chalet with an injury suffered on the slopes. Russell's first impressions of Diana were not positive. Though he liked the future princess, he delved into her inner self and found a young woman still troubled by her past rather than brimming with optimism about her future. He recalled her giggling and making a snide comment to him upon her arrival, which turned him off. Russell perceived her as unconfident, though he believed she should have enjoyed a great deal of self-assuredness. After spending more time with Diana, he saw a young woman happy on the outside, but tortured on the inside by her parents' divorce. Diana needed a sense of accomplishment both personally and professionally.

She received both through the workings of her family. Sister Sarah, who had landed a job at Savills, a prominent real estate agency, found a luxurious apartment that her parents bought for Diana for her 18th birthday. Diana soon fulfilled a promise to school chum Carolyn Bartholomew that they would become roommates as soon as the opportunity presented itself. Fellow friends Sophie Kimball and Philippa Coaker moved in briefly, but were soon replaced by Virginia Pittman and Anne Bolton, who worked with Sarah at Savills. The quartet enjoyed themselves immensely. They filled their free time with laughter and innocent fun. Even a burglary that cost Diana a great deal of her jewelry didn't put much of a damper on the joy she received from such youthful pursuits. And for the first time in her young adult life, Diana developed a sense of pride in the apartment—her own possession—even though her parents had purchased it. She used the skills received during her brief stint in cooking school to whip up culinary specialties such as Russian borscht soup and chocolate roulades, though the cooking of full dinners by any of the four was rare. As the landlady, Diana charged her roommates rent and established a cleaning rotation among them. She left no uncertainty as to who was in charge when she emblazoned the words "Chief Chick" on the door of her bedroom, which was the largest in the apartment. Bartholomew recalled that Diana felt strongly about having her own home, which motivated the future princess to move about the place wearing rubber gloves for cleaning.

It was at this time that Diana found a job in which she could thrive. She landed a part-time teaching position at the Young England kindergarten. She instructed the children on painting, drawing, and dancing so well that Victoria Wilson and Kay Seth-Smith, who ran the school, added hours to her schedule. Diana also enjoyed her work caring for the young son of an American oil executive one afternoon a week.

Diana tried to foster a better relationship with Sarah and earn extra money at the same time by helping clean her sister's home in Chelsea. She played the role of Cinderella by getting on her hands and knees and scrubbing the floor, as well as doing various other household chores for little money. Lucinda Craig Harvey, who shared the flat with Sarah, believed her roommate was taking advantage of Diana. Harvey claimed that Sarah told her not to be embarrassed when she asked Diana to do menial household chores. The drudgery of performing such tasks was one reason why Diana so enjoyed her free time with her roommates. They embarked on such juvenile pranks as calling people saddled with strange names they found in the phone book. They even plopped eggs and flour on the car of one boy who had disappointed Diana on a date.

There were many dates, some of whom had been cast aside by Sarah. Young men found Diana attractive both physically and spiritually. They enjoyed her often-absurd sense of humor. But when they attempted to take the relationship further, Diana backed away. She felt a sense of destiny in her life, which translated into maintaining her virginity. Bartholomew expressed her belief during Diana's marriage to Prince Charles that a guiding force played a role in cementing that relationship. Bartholomew offered that a spiritual feeling held by Diana prevented her from allowing men to go further physically.[1] She was keeping herself "pure" for the man of her destiny, much to the dismay of the young men who were attracted to the pretty, shapely Diana. Among them was Rory Scott, who later lamented that his relationship with the future princess remained platonic despite his attraction to her. He felt a bit distant from her throughout their time together.

Was she indeed saving herself for Prince Charles? Such feelings would have likely been premature for two reasons. First, she had yet to establish anything more than a friendship with him. Second, he was inundated with potential queens-to-be. Some were sincere in their feelings for the prince, but others simply dreamed of wearing the crown. Diana looked up to the prince, as one might expect from any teenager in Britain at the time. But after having spent more than just fleeting moments with him, she had developed a desire to mother him. She was deeply sympathetic when Irish Republican Army radicals planted a bomb that killed Earl Mountbatten, his father's uncle and life mentor with whom Charles had forged a close relationship.

LOVE LIFE OF A PRINCE

Charles had all that he could handle from the opposite sex. Among his suitors was Lady Amanda Knatchbull, the granddaughter of the assassinated earl, who had played the role of matchmaker. The couple remained together after the murder, which fueled speculation that a wedding was imminent. Perhaps it would have been, had Earl Mountbatten remained alive to see the relationship through. But Amanda rejected the notion of losing her privacy as a member of the royal family, which ended such speculation. The two maintained a friendship, however, for several years thereafter.

The same couldn't be said for Anna Wallace, a young Scottish woman who attracted the attention of Prince Charles during a foxhunting trip in late 1979. Most observers believe Amanda Knatchbull would have been received with open arms, but they felt quite the opposite about Wallace, who was feisty and headstrong. Despite that view, the prince continued dating Wallace. But her overzealous attitude finally wore thin, particularly when he ignored her during a ball at Windsor Castle marking the Queen Mother's 80th birthday. She fumed when he danced with another woman that evening. Her anger mounted when he did the same at their next public appearance, and she stormed out. Within a month, she had married another.

The woman with whom Prince Charles danced the night away on both occasions was Camilla Parker Bowles, with whom he had been infatuated for years. He was 23 years old when he met then Camilla Shand in 1971. Highly intelligent, well educated, witty, and exceptionally attractive, Shand proved to be an immediate attraction for the young prince. The royal history of England might have been quite different had Shand not already been involved with Andrew Parker Bowles, a dashing officer in the Household Cavalry who was a decade older than his rival. He was also a bit more serious about tying the knot than Prince Charles, who spent a great deal of time with Camilla in 1972, but was not yet searching for a wife.

The prince faced an eight-month excursion at sea with the Royal Navy in early 1973. Midway through his stint he learned that Camilla had become engaged to Parker Bowles. The couple wed that July. By that time, Prince Charles had turned his attention to Knatchbull. Yet three years later, when he left the Royal Navy, he was no closer to marriage than he had been at age 23. The prince was understandably quite picky. After all, whomever he asked to be his bride was destined to be queen of England. It was such thoughts that washed over him even back in 1969 during a television interview. The woman he married not only had to serve as his soulmate but also had to live up to royal standards. He told reporters that he understood the importance of his choice for a bride, which caused him to consider carefully. Even the media, he surmised, would expect much from his decision. Prince Charles spoke often about distinguishing between women who truly loved him and women who simply put on an act because of their desire to be queen. His yearning to be married had to coincide with finding a woman who wished to remain wed until "death do you part." While friends and members of the royal family urged him to find a suitable match, he continued to state that it simply wasn't that easy.

"My marriage has to be forever," he told Kenneth Harris in an article in the *Observor* on January 7, 1975.

> A lot of people get the wrong idea of what love is all about. It is rather more than just falling madly in love with somebody and having a love affair for the rest of your married life. It's basically a very strong friendship. As often as not you have shared interests and ideas in common also have a great deal of affection. And I think where you are very lucky is when you find the person attractive in the physical and the mental sense. To me marriage . . . seems to be one of the biggest and

most responsible steps to be taken in one's life. . . . Marriage is
something you ought to work at. I may easily be proved wrong
but I intend to work at it when I get married.

Lord Mountbatten had placed in the mind of Prince Charles what
some would consider a hypocritical view of the ideal relationship between
the prince and his potential mate. It reinforced many of Charles's notions
about what he was looking for. "I believe in a case like yours, the man
should sow his wild oats and have as many affairs as he can before settling
down, but for a wife he should choose a suitable, attractive and sweet-
charactered girl before she has met anyone else she might fall for," he
wrote to Charles. "I think it is disturbing for women to have experiences
if they have to remain on a pedestal after marriage."[2]

The prince had still not settled on a suitable lifelong mate in 1979,
when he again struck up a relationship with Camilla Parker Bowles. He
poured his heart and soul out to Camilla, speaking to her about his anxieties over finding a prospective wife, among other things. She was open to
a closer bond with the prince, particularly since she believed her husband
had strayed often. Camilla and the prince leaped at the opportunity to
spend time together when Andrew left for a six-month business trip to
Rhodesia (now Zimbabwe). They quickly fell in love, but relationships
involving Prince Charles were difficult to hide. Friends and royal family
members warned him that an affair with a married woman could ruin his
reputation. Andrew Parker Bowles didn't seem to mind. He watched with
no jealousy as the prince kissed his wife passionately on the dance floor at
a polo ball in 1980.

Charles himself didn't necessarily want to wed, but he felt that he was
being forced to. The murder of Earl Mountbatten, who had strongly believed that the prince needed to find a bride, weighed heavily in his heart
and on his mind in July 1980, when both he and Diana were invited to
stay the weekend at the home of a common friend. After watching the
prince play polo, Diana sidled up to him on a bale of hay during a barbe-
cue and spoke thoughtfully about the death of Earl Mountbatten and the
effect she perceived it had on him. She told him that she was troubled by
his sadness at the funeral and that he needed somebody to take care of
him emotionally. Diana's words touched at his heartstrings. But there was
another reaction she neither expected nor welcomed. She reported later
that he leaped on her, which took her aback. She was too young and inexperienced to act otherwise. She pulled away, yet Charles still asked her to
travel with him to London the next day. He told her of his need to work at
Buckingham Palace, but she turned down his invitation.

The prince apparently wasn't simply looking to advance his physical relationship with Diana. He invited her to join him on his royal yacht *Britannia* for a week of sailing. According to Prince Charles's official biographer Jonathan Dimbleby, he stunned a close friend by implying that he had finally met the woman he planned on marrying and praised Diana for her warmth and easygoing style.[3] The prince felt a sense of security when those close to him raved about Diana. Among them was Patti Palmer-Tomkinson, whose husband Charles was among his closest friends. Palmer-Tomkinson was immediately taken by Diana's outgoing personality and ability to laugh at herself. On one occasion she fell into a bog and was covered with mud, but rather than rise angrily, she laughed heartily. Parker-Tomkinson detected in her an openness to new experiences, as well as an intense interest in the prince.

The budding romance picked up steam in September, when Charles invited Diana to join him at Balmoral, Queen Elizabeth's Highland castle retreat, for the Braemar Games. Diana was overwhelmed by the social expectations of the royal family. Passing such a test required far more knowledge of social traditions than were ever taught at West Heath. Her fears were quelled a bit when she learned she would be staying in a cottage on the estate rather than in the main house. Prince Charles, however, didn't treat her like a secondary guest. He invited her to spend time with him daily.

Diana even impressed none other than the Queen Mother, with whom she stayed during a visit to Scotland in October while Prince Charles was away. That the Queen Mother had invited Diana to spend time with her was considered a telling sign that the royal family believed she was not only a suitable partner for the prince but potential queen material.

FATAL ATTRACTION

Diana reveled in the attention, and her feelings for the prince continued to grow. The media attention, however, proved more than disconcerting. On one occasion, tabloid photographers followed the couple to a river where Charles was fishing. Uneducated about the persistence of such journalists, she scampered behind a tree in the blind hope they would leave. The photographers continued to take pictures in a vain attempt to discover her identity, but Diana hid her face and escaped through the woods.

Such clever methods of maintaining her privacy couldn't last long. Soon, reporters were regularly camping outside her apartment for a glimpse and a word with the young woman they now considered the most likely candidate to join Prince Charles in holy matrimony. They tormented her by gathering outside the Young England kindergarten. The hounding unnerved Diana, but she never let it show to members of the press, to whom she was friendly while giving them no juicy tidbits about her relationship with the prince. Neither he nor the royal family made an effort to stem the tide, perhaps because they believed such media attention was inevitable and they were curious about how Diana would handle it.

What angered Diana was that Charles appeared more concerned about the plight of Camilla than about her own problems. He spoke sympathetically about Camilla dealing with several journalists camping outside her home, and he ignored Diana's pleas regarding far greater annoyances. But Diana said nothing. She had fallen in love with the prince and didn't want to rock the boat. Although there were dozens of media members camped outside her own apartment, Diana never raised those concerns with the prince. She would have considered having just four journalists outside her home a private moment. Media members didn't simply plant themselves on Coleherne Court or at her place of work. They followed Diana wherever she went. She sometimes felt compelled to escape, which she did when driving. She often zipped through a light just as it was turning red, forcing reporters who were following her to stop. On one occasion, when she was leaving her home to join Charles at Broadlands, she escaped out the kitchen window to avoid the crush of reporters, to whom she remained polite. She admitted that she shed many a tear over her predicament and complained that she didn't get any help from the royal family.

Diana also didn't want to make waves about Charles's relationship with Camilla, which made her uneasy as well. Diana wondered why Camilla knew intimate details about her relationship with the prince. And rarely did Charles invite Diana to any function without the Parker-Bowleses tagging along. Diana's desire to be alone with him often went unfulfilled. Yet the prince did show that he had designs on Diana as a future wife. He showed her around his mansion in Gloucestershire, then asked her to map out plans for its interior decoration. She felt the request was rather premature considering they had yet to become engaged.

Despite the ongoing relationship between the prince and Camilla, the latter strongly encouraged him to propose to Diana. Many friends believed that Camilla hoped to continue holding a passionate place in Charles's life and figured that would be made easier if he married a young, timid woman with little experience in romance. Yet neither Diana's nagging doubts about Charles's feelings toward Camilla nor the constant hounding by the British press could discourage her. She was like a blushing schoolgirl around the prince, whom she deeply admired. The fact that she had never had a boyfriend played a role in her giddiness over being the chosen woman of the Prince of Wales.

She officially became engaged on February 6, 1981. Charles proposed to Diana after returning from a skiing trip. Diana responded by giggling. The prince reiterated his proposal, emphasizing its seriousness with a reminder that she would someday be queen. She answered that she would indeed marry him and spoke of her love for him. He then responded with a curious phrase that would put to question his feelings for her. The prince replied, "Whatever love means" and went off to phone the queen.[4] They were the same words he reiterated during interviews with the media regarding the engagement.

Soon thereafter, Diana took a three-week trip to Australia with her mother to start planning the wedding, but it proved to be a haunting portent of things to come in terms of her relationship with the prince. She seemed to miss him far more than he missed her. She considered it both odd and sadly foreboding that he didn't return her phone calls.

It wouldn't be the last time Diana questioned Charles's feelings for her. In fact, the issue would ruin her married life.

NOTES

1. Sarah Bradford, *Diana* (New York: Viking Press, 2006), 47.

2. Penny Junor, *The Firm, The Troubled Life of the House of Windsor* (New York: St. Martin's Press, 2005), 72.

3. Tim Clayton and Phil Craig, *Diana: Story of a Princess* (New York: Simon and Schuster, 2001), 36.

4. Andrew Morton, *Diana: Her True Story* (New York: Simon and Schuster, 1997), 116.

Chapter 5

THE ENGAGEMENT

Both Diana and Charles were immature in matters of the heart. Diana had little experience in relationships with the opposite sex. She had remained a virgin with the notion that by remaining "pure" she would please Charles and the royal family. Charles, on the other hand, had been pushed by the Queen Mother and others to tie the knot. It is widely believed he married Diana more because friends and family felt a commitment to wed was overdue and not because he felt a sincere, passionate love for her.

Meanwhile, Diana's friends and most of her family were celebrating with the belief that she was to be a happy fairy tale princess, but Frances suspected otherwise. She was alone among Diana's inner circle to warn her against the marriage. During the trip with her daughter to Australia, she brought up her concerns. Perhaps Frances noticed similarities to her early relationship with Johnnie. She felt that Diana was too young to jump into wedlock and that there was too great an age gap between her and the prince. How would Diana feel when she got a bit older and wanted to spread her wings and realize her full potential? Frances had experienced identical feelings. She didn't want Diana to make the same mistake.

Among the priorities of Prince Charles during his search for a bride was to find a woman whose desire to marry him far outweighed her yearning to be queen. Considering such a prerequisite, Diana was an ideal choice—at least that was the view of her brother, who sensed her unbridled joy and enthusiasm when she informed her family of the engagement the day after the prince popped the question. Charles recalled that his sister looked and acted thrilled over the engagement. He also got the impression that she felt she could handle the intense media scrutiny. Diana's roommates at Coleherne Court shared her joy. She didn't want her relationship with them to change. She didn't want to change herself. But she did want to involve them in the excitement. When news about the engagement appeared on TV, she would call out to her friends, "Come quick, they're talking about us on the telly!"[1]

That sweet nectar of joy would soon drain away. Diana moved into Buckingham Palace, where she felt isolated, even imprisoned. Despite her aristocratic upbringing and training, she felt out of place socializing with the royal family and their friends, many of whom she considered stuffy and dull. The pressure from all sides was closing in. How would she handle the overwhelming media attention? How would she handle the expectations of being a princess and future queen? Were her freedom and privacy gone forever? Such questions haunted Diana. She was performing a role with little assuredness. In a moment, she had gone from little-known teenager to lead character of a fairy tale watched by the world.

It was at this time that the disease that inflicted sister Sarah began taking a toll on her as well. The healthy Diana, who was chased by young men throughout London, became painfully thin, courtesy of bulimia nervosa. Her waist size shrunk from 29 inches to 23½ inches during the five months between the day her engagement was announced and the day of the wedding. Her friends couldn't help but notice. Bartholomew recalled Diana's sadness and weight loss upon her move to Buckingham Palace, both of which greatly concerned her. She saw a Diana who was simply overwhelmed by the pressure from all sides. Diana was torn between gorging on three meals a day and cake with her midafternoon tea and slimming down for the cameras. She was terrified at the notion of being a fat princess, especially in an era when fashion models were painfully thin. So she purged her food, which allowed her to satisfy everyone but herself.

Few others, least of all members of the royal family, knew of her misery. The Queen Mother had been particularly aggressive in her push to have the prince propose to Diana. Now that it was done, all appeared well on both sides of the family. Robert Spencer, Johnnie's cousin and close confidante, saw nothing but acceptance and joyful anticipation. "I don't remember any reservations at that time at all," he said.

> I remember just celebrating, because it did appear then how eminently suitable Diana was. She'd never had any serious affairs, she was 19-and-a-half, extremely beautiful and most popular, and she seemed to share interests with the Prince of Wales. She gave the impression of loving the country life, in particular staying at Balmoral. She seemed to be madly in

love with him and, after all, she did come from stock of a family who had worked with and supported the Royal Family for many generations. And it seemed ever more suitable because the Prince seemed like somebody who would want a younger girl to be his wife. She was young enough to be trained, and young enough to be helped, and young enough to be molded.[2]

GAMES PEOPLE PLAY

One activity in which Diana and Prince Charles didn't share a fondness was hunting. For reasons unknown to Diana at the time, that fact was quite interesting to Camilla Parker Bowles. Camilla and Diana had met for lunch shortly after the engagement announcement. The meeting was precipitated by Camilla, who invited the princess-to-be while the prince was on an official trip to Australia and New Zealand. During lunch, Camilla pressed Diana about her plans to join her husband on hunting expeditions. She appeared quite relieved when Diana told her she had no desire to do so. It wasn't until later that Diana realized that Camilla was finding out when she could have Charles to herself.

"We had lunch and, bearing in mind that I was so immature, I didn't know about jealousy or depressions or anything like that," Diana recalled.

I had a wonderful existence being a kindergarten teacher—you didn't suffer from anything like that, you got tired but that was it. There was no one around to give you grief. So we had lunch. Very tricky indeed. She said, "You are not going to hunt, are you?" I said, "On what?" She said, "Horse. You are not going to hunt when you go and live at Highgrove, are you?" I said, "No." She said, "I just wanted to know" and I thought as far as she was concerned that was her communication route. Still too immature to understand all the messages coming my way.[3]

Prince Charles was sending messages as well, though not always intentionally. Diana once overheard him on the phone telling Camilla that his love for her would never die. Diana informed him that she had been listening at the door, which precipitated a heated argument. She reversed her shy and demure image on her first public date with Prince Charles since the engagement was announced by slipping on a sexy black dress that showed a great deal of cleavage from a busty young woman. And though wearing such tantalizing clothing did not fit the royal image and black was generally worn only in mourning, Diana's point to both Charles and Camilla was unmistakable. It was a coming-out party of sorts, one that tried to reveal Diana as a teenager in years only. She could do no more than dress with confidence. During a visit to the powder room on that very occasion, she shared her insecurities with Princess Grace. The reply was good-natured, but not one that would alleviate Diana's doubts. "Don't worry," Grace told her. "It will get a lot worse."[4]

Any suspicions Diana might have had about Camilla and Charles at the time had plenty of time to fester in her mind. The royal family had given little thought to what role to give her beyond that of princess. She was tremendously bored during much of her engagement as the people around her at Buckingham Palace went about their business. She felt as if the life that made her feel productive and happy had been snatched away from her. She was no longer Diana Spencer, but rather an unhappy captive in a fairy tale. Diana missed hanging out with her friends and such things as borrowing clothes from them and gossiping about unimportant happenings. She was no longer in her comfort zone. She felt that the official company at Buckingham Palace was cold and impersonal.

In response, she turned her attention to the palace staff, to whom she felt a far greater kinship. Though having been raised in an aristocratic setting, she had always been more comfortable around commoners. She developed a bond with Michael Colborne, private secretary to the prince, who met Diana before the engagement and was immediately struck by her desire to relate to him on the same level rather than as a possible queen of England. She asked if she could call him by his given first name, and he assured her that she could, but that he could only refer to her as "Ma'am." The two got along quite well. They shared an office from the engagement to the wedding and discussed many subjects. Colborne recalled that Diana was often sad when he left for lunch.

Meanwhile, Diana tried to occupy her time in her palace suite, which consisted of a bedroom, bathroom, sitting room, and small kitchen. She was provided with two servants, whom she rarely needed. Diana whiled away the hours by shopping and running errands for the wedding, watching soap operas, and reliving her past by tap dancing. When she did make appearances at particular functions, she felt woefully lacking in the social graces required of her. She later expressed a lack of schooling by the palace staff about such fundamental skills as whether to enter a room before or after the prince. Charles's biographer Jonathan Dimbleby, who offered quite a different recollection, refuted that claim. "[Several advisors tried to] instruct her in the ways of the court and what they saw as her duties," Dimbleby remembered. "They explained that her future role as consort . . . would be more complicated than she might have realized, and that her husband would not be at her side as often as either of them might have wished. They also told her that . . . she would always be expected to walk somewhat in his shadow."[5]

Diana was taught such niceties as the curtsy and the "royal wave," which consisted of a raised hand, cupped forward and swiveling from side to side. She was instructed by Prince Charles to keep herself fresh in a crowd by shaking hands with every fifteenth person and to smile pleasantly when avoiding answering a pointed question. The amount of schooling she received on the proper etiquette of royalty has been debated, as well as how much she was expected to learn on her own. A more mature and assured woman might have wrested control of the situation, but the 19-year-old Diana was still neither.

She was also unable to confidently approach Charles's relationship with Camilla. The prince told Diana of the relationship, but he assured his bride that she would be the only woman in his life. It has been offered that a more trusting Diana might have inspired his loyalty. Instead, she attempted in vain to convince him to sell his Highgrove country home, located a mere 11 miles from Camilla's house.

Diana's suspicions were raised again just two weeks before the wedding when she opened a package addressed to Camilla sitting on Colborne's desk. Despite protests from the prince's private secretary, she opened it and found a bracelet bearing an inscription with the initials G. F., which she knew stood for Charles's nickname for Camilla: "Girl Friday." Diana ran out of the office in tears. She confronted Charles, who informed her it was a present to be given to Camilla at a lunch signifying their parting of ways on July 27, two days before the wedding. But Diana suspected there would be no goodbyes between Camilla and the prince. While Charles was dining with Camilla, Diana was lunching with her sisters, who told her it was too late to back out of the wedding.

Throughout the engagement, Diana searched for sympathetic ears. One of them was Queen Elizabeth II, who enjoyed her company and eagerly agreed to dine with her quite often. "Will the Queen be dining alone today?" Diana would timidly ask a staff member over the phone. When informed of the request, the queen would invariably reply, "Oh, do ask her to join me."[6] Diana's feelings for Queen Elizabeth II transformed from royal respect to a sincere affection, particularly since she was always accommodating during troubled times. Diana saw in the queen a woman who had adapted to the trials and protocols of royalty just as she would have to do. And it appeared that the queen had more faith in Diana's ability to make that transition than did her son.

Even the simplest routines caused an uproar. One weekend day Diana went for a short stroll, and all hell broke loose due to security concerns.

She related the story to Colborne the following Monday, whereupon he gave her ample warning about her future as Princess of Wales. "This is going to be your life," Colborne said. "You're never going to be on your own again. And you're going to change. In four to five years you're going to be an absolute bitch, not through any fault of your own, but because of the circumstances in which you live. If you want four boiled eggs for breakfast, you'll have them. If you want the car brought round to the front door a minute ago, you'll have it. It's going to change you."[7]

BINGING AND PURGING

The tremendous stress felt by Diana as the wedding approached heightened her bulimia. It wasn't until much later that she fully understood the reasons behind her overeating and purging. The tension was only part of it. "When you have bulimia you're very ashamed of yourself and you hate yourself, so—and people think you're wasting food, so you don't discuss it with people," Diana said. "The thing about bulimia is your weight always stays the same, whereas with anorexia you visibly shrink. So (with bulimia) you can pretend the whole way through. There's no proof." Yet there was indeed proof. Diana lost 14 pounds in the four months leading up to the ceremony. She herself admitted, "I had shrunk to nothing."[8] One reason for the weight loss was that Diana wasn't only bulimic. Her obsession with her appearance prompted several episodes of fasting. Though her bulimia was more pronounced, her overall unhealthy eating habits caused by both her stress and her still-poor self-image played a huge role in the quite-noticeable weight plunge.

Though Frances spent more time with Diana during the engagement than she had in several years and was aware of her daughter's bulimia, she declined to become involved. Diana's mother had experienced eating disorders of her own, and she also knew of Sarah's bouts with bulimia. Frances has been criticized for her passive attitude toward Diana's problems at the time. She admitted that she knew immediately that her daughter had an eating disorder, especially since she had dealt with the same disease with Sarah. But she didn't want to become too involved for fear of accentuating the problem and even worsening it.

Diana felt alone. Her family members were basking in the glow of their future relationship with the royal family, though Sarah remained bitter toward her for marrying a man with whom she was once involved. Diana no longer shared close ties with her Coleherne Court friends. She had nobody in whom to confide her anxieties. Johnnie and Raine spoke glowingly about Diana to the media. They mistakenly praised her ability to adapt easily to the role of princess. Some of that optimism might have been a whistle in the dark, but Diana hadn't confided in them about her deepest fears.

Two public appearances shortly before the wedding illustrated her conflicting public persona. The first was a royal ball that Charles threw for family and friends at Buckingham Palace. The festive evening showed Diana in high spirits, though she admitted to being an emotional wreck as the ceremony approached. She spent much time dancing with young men with whom she had become acquainted at Coleherne Court, such as Rory Scott. Her stress appeared far more prevalent when she showed up to watch Charles play polo at Windsor Great Park—their last public appearance together before the wedding. In attendance were 20,000 people, many of whom came not to catch a glimpse of the prince swinging the royal mallet, but to view his bride-to-be. It was hardly an encouraging sight. John Edwards of the *Daily Mirror* reported on July 27, 1981, "Her face was pale and grey as limestone and she hardly smiled. She ran out of Prince Charles's open Aston Martin before the car had actually stopped. She went straight to the shelter of the Queen's private chalet and stayed there twisting a white cardigan in her hands, peeping nervously from behind the door at the crowds and not wanting to join them. A few days seemed to have changed her. Her bounce was gone. The quips stayed buried. She had shed weight and was uneasy with the crush all around her."[9]

Although Diana felt as though her fate was out of her hands, she maintained a shred of control by ignoring Charles's wishes and choosing her own dressmakers for the big event. They were David and Elizabeth Emanuel, a young couple who was quite inexperienced in the art, particularly in creating a masterpiece for one of the most storied weddings in history. Diana figured that if the fairy tale wasn't going according to plan, the historic dress was going to fit the fairy tale image. She even had the Emanuels place a diamond-studded horseshoe in the waistband for good luck. Diana also insisted on puffy sleeves and floating silk and a 25-foot taffeta train with antique lace embroidered with sequins and pearls. She pictured the frilly dress transporting her from her pained existence into a world of love and optimism as her father escorted her down the aisle.

Though Diana had spoken about being sick after a bulimic episode on the eve of the wedding, those close to her told a quite different story. Among them was William Tallon, the elderly page for the Queen Mother. Tallon saw what he believed to be a lighthearted, optimistic, and joyous Diana when he invited her into his office for a friendly chat. "She saw my bicycle standing against a wall and she got on it and started to ride round and round," Tallon recalled. "(She was) ringing the bell singing, 'I'm going to marry the Prince of Wales tomorrow.' Ring, ring. 'I'm going to marry the Prince of Wales tomorrow!' Ring, ring! I can hear that bicycle ringing now. She was just a child you know, just a little girl."[10]

Diana became quite the expert, however, at hiding her unhappiness. She admitted to falling apart during the wedding rehearsal at storied St. Paul's Cathedral, but the tears must have been shed in private, for friends and family members didn't detect any problems. Diana did admit to collapsing emotionally, however, due to her jealousy and mistrust of Camilla throughout the engagement and her own inability to deal with it. Yet, Sarah Jane Gaselee, who was 11 years old at the time and served as a bridesmaid, believed Diana was feeling quite the opposite from watching the soon-to-be princess at the rehearsal dinner. "I don't think she was stressed by it or anything," Gaselee remembered years later. "It didn't appear that way. What I do remember is that she and Charles were really in love as far as I could see, at that age. I saw them cuddling on the sofa and during the rehearsals they had their arms linked and were skipping down the aisles. It was all really happy, or so I thought."[11]

Diana appeared to be soothed at the time by a token of love she received from Charles that day, which she spent at Clarence House. The prince sent her a signet ring, engraved with the Prince of Wales feathers, and a note that read, "I'm so proud of you and when you come up I'll be there at the altar for you tomorrow. Just look 'em in the eye and knock 'em dead."[12] Though such a message wasn't exactly filled with romance and feelings of love, it did calm Diana. But she was too calm. She was numbed by the reality of her situation. Diana spoke of herself as a helpless lamb heading to slaughter.

Diana awoke early on her wedding day—July 29, 1981—to the festive sounds of the huge crowd that had gathered outside Clarence House. The scene from the movie *The Graduate* featuring the bride bolting down the aisle and running out of the church popped into her mind. Would she still feel like a lamb heading to its slaughter when the wedding bells rang? Or would she experience an intense love for Charles and be brimming with hope? Even she didn't know as the world eagerly awaited the Wedding of the Century.

NOTES

1. Martine Kurz and Christine Gaughey, *Diana: A Princess for the World* (Paris: Editions de la Martiniere, 1997), 17.

2. Tim Clayton and Phil Craig, *Diana: Story of a Princess* (New York: Simon and Schuster, 2001), 56.

3. Andrew Morton, *Diana: Her True Story* (New York: Simon and Schuster, 1997), 38.

4. Tina Brown, *The Diana Chronicles* (New York: Doubleday, 2007), 158.

5. Sally Bedell Smith, *Diana in Search of Herself* (New York: Times Books, 1999), 102.

6. Paul Burrell, *A Royal Duty* (New York: G. P. Putnam's Sons, 2003), 57.

7. Penny Junor, *The Firm, The Troubled Life of the House of Windsor* (New York: St. Martin's Press, 2005), 66.

8. Smith, *Diana in Search of Herself,* 110.

9. Quoted in Brown, *The Diana Chronicles,* 162–63.

10. Ibid., 168–69.

11. Sarah Bradford, *Diana* (New York: Viking Press, 2006), 89.

12. Morton, *Diana: Her True Story,* 125.

Chapter 6

THE WEDDING

Diana felt tremendous internal pressure leading up to the wedding. But the external factors would have made anyone nervous. It was, after all, to be a worldwide event at the hallowed St. Paul's Cathedral. Not only were 3,500 people invited, but 2 million spectators gathered along the procession route, overwhelming both Diana and her father. Another 750 million throughout the world watched the wedding on television. Add the radio listeners, and those tuning in numbered around a billion. The expectations of Diana extended beyond the role of fairy tale princess for a day. She was to be the first British citizen to wed an heir to the throne since the 1600s.

Conflicting thoughts occupied Diana's mind throughout her wedding day, which she began by watching television coverage of the massive crowd outside. The Emanuels dressed her in her ivory silk dress and tiara before she left for Buckingham Palace, where a glass coach was to whisk Diana and Johnnie away to St. Paul's Cathedral. The end of her 25-foot train had to be placed on her lap. The fairy tale day had begun, and she was enjoying every moment.

Prince Charles awoke to the buzz of anticipation created by the huge throng outside Buckingham Palace. He soaked in the sight of 150 Union Jack flags bedecking the mall flagstaffs and flowers decorating the lampposts. Every building in sight displayed red, white, and blue banners and bunting. The crowd gazed at Buckingham Palace, cheering at every sign of life. Soon a procession of black limousines carrying royal family members from around the world was rolling along toward St. Paul's Cathedral.

Meanwhile, Diana and Johnnie waved enthusiastically as they drove through crowds of people jamming the procession route. People tossed flowers at the coach or shouted congratulatory words as she rolled by. The noise became so loud and distracting that Johnnie mistook St. Martin's-in-the-Fields Cathedral in Trafalgar Square for St. Paul's and nearly exited the coach. Only quick reflexes by Diana, who held her father back, prevented him from getting out. The enormous, giddy reaction from her fellow Britons thrilled Diana. Their smiles were infectious. She felt a kinship with the people and optimism for the future. She had believed throughout the engagement that her importance as a princess would be as a link to the public, not as a figurehead or symbol of the royal family. Many girls and young women had already adopted her hairstyle and style of dress.

After Diana emerged from the coach in front of the cathedral, the Emanuels raced to spread out her train, which had become quite wrinkled in the coach. It flowed beautifully as she walked up the carpeted steps. "She was extremely gentle, very shy, and she was someone that as a young girl you thought was everything a princess should be," remembered India Hicks, a 10-year-old bridesmaid at the time. "Very beautiful, very young, very calm—and yet there was a kind of nervousness about her. But the feeling inside the cathedral was just enormous. It's a very hollow place but it was filled with so much warmth and excitement."[1]

Diana walked slowly down the aisle, mindful of her father's fragile physical state. She noted various guests, particularly Camilla, whom she spotted in a pale gray, veiled pillbox hat. It was the only time she saw Camilla that day, for Diana had made certain she was not invited to the postwedding luncheon. Diana no longer felt anger or jealousy, thinking instead that any romantic relationship between Camilla and Charles was over. When she sidled up to the prince at the altar, a love for him washed over her. "I remember being so in love with my husband that I couldn't take my eyes off him," Diana recalled. "I just absolutely thought I was the luckiest girl in the world." He whispered, "You look beautiful" to Diana, who replied sweetly, "Beautiful for you."[2]

Diana later expressed a quite opposite memory of her emotions years after the wedding. Her words help explain the conflicting feelings racing through her head: "The day I walked down the aisle at St. Paul's Cathedral, I felt that my personality was taken away from me, and I was taken over by the royal machine."[3] Those words might have been a product of Diana's bitterness after her relationship with Charles had ended. There appeared little doubt on her wedding day that she felt a tremendous passion for her husband and a strong sense of optimism for the future. She later planted a kiss on Charles's lips on the Buckingham Palace balcony, which drew a roar of approval from the huge, adoring crowd.

NO HEAVENLY HONEYMOON

By the end of the day, Diana was ready to get away from the cheering throngs, flashing cameras, and media requests. She yearned to be alone with Prince Charles, and she thought she would receive that opportunity on a two-week honeymoon cruise of the Mediterranean on his royal yacht *Brittania*. No longer would she have to compete with his work schedule. No longer would the press interrupt her time with him. She simply couldn't wait.

But soon all her dreams of a fairy tale honeymoon, of being alone with her husband, of simply feeling happy, were dashed. The couple left for Broadlands, which had been the home of Lord Mountbatten. It was on the honeymoon that all the fears and anxieties she had felt during the engagement returned. She became overwhelmed by the permanence of her situation. She noticed during a dinner with Egyptian president Anwar Sadat that Charles was wearing cufflinks with intertwined Cs (which stood for Charles and Camilla) that had been presented to him by Camilla in defiance of Diana's wishes, which further angered and depressed her. Her inexperience as a lover and what she perceived as his inability and even unwillingness to please her left them both wanting romantically.

Princess Diana lamented that she had entered her marriage with hope, but the hope was gone within a couple of days. She complained about the need to entertain the staff of the *Brittania*, which left her little time to spend with Charles. She was undergoing horrible bulimic episodes several times a day, eating as much as she could, then purging just minutes later. She recalled crying often on her honeymoon and being tired for all the wrong reasons.

The couple went straight to their destination after getting off the yacht. They received a tremendous welcome, but in later years, Diana expressed a more vivid recollection of terrible nightmares starring Camilla. Her mistrust of her husband and Camilla had reached its zenith. At Balmoral, she felt like an untouchable figure and remembered the staff treating her with kid gloves. Diana simply wanted to be treated as the young woman she knew herself to be, rather than treated as a glass figurine. Her jealousy of Camilla was understandable—even before she spotted the cufflinks on Charles, two photographs of Camilla dropped out of his diary when he and Diana were looking through it. She began to cry, begging him to give her a straight answer about his feelings toward Camilla. He ignored those pleas.

The clash in personality and interests between Diana and Charles became apparent during the honeymoon. So did the vast age difference. The prince was most comfortable fishing or reading. He pursued intellectual stimulation from authors such as mystical philosopher Laurens van der Post and psychoanalyst Carl Jung. He attempted to share with Diana his fascination with both, but she simply wasn't ready mentally or emotionally to soak in the knowledge. Some have speculated that her poor academic history translated into a weak intellectual self-image. Diana, meanwhile, spent much of her time with the crew, with whom she had more fun. She even thrilled the sailors with an impromptu performance on the piano. Diana would have preferred spending more time with her new husband, but Charles hoped she would develop an interest in what he enjoyed. When it became apparent that he wasn't about to give her his undivided attention, Diana felt spurned. Meanwhile, her weight dropped to 110 pounds.

She began to discover the merit of her mother's warnings. Frances always felt much younger than Johnnie in both outlook and age. She had married too young and had eventually become antsy to go her own way. Diana was not old enough and hadn't been with Charles long enough to lose her emotional attachment to him, but she was feeling the effects of their differences in attitude and age. Her boredom had become pronounced early in the trip. She was a young woman who enjoyed the sun and the water, but such activities were unavailable on the boat. When they did reach ports of call, dignitaries such as Sadat took up their time. Diana would have preferred a bit of shopping, but the crowds besieging them precluded such activity. So she found entertainment wherever she could. While Charles relaxed on the deck with a book, she showed up unexpectedly and surprisingly to party with the crewmen, who wondered what she was doing there. Neither Charles nor Diana could identify with the other. It was a mismatch from the start, a fact both were becoming painfully aware of. "Diana dashes about chatting up all the sailors and cooks in the galley, etc., while I remain hermit-like on the verandah deck, sunk with pure joy into one of Laurens van der Post's books," Charles wrote to friends from the *Brittania*.[4]

Diana's unhappiness both frightened and frustrated Charles. He had no answers. He pleaded with her to cheer up, but to no avail. She wanted him near, but remaining close to his unhappy wife wasn't his idea of fun and it certainly didn't seem to help. Yet when he left her alone, she felt abandoned. Charles felt sorry for her, but he had always preferred strong women in his life. Diana's weaknesses only served to prevent his feelings for her to grow. He felt suffocated by her emotional needs and couldn't honestly tell her what she wanted to hear—that he loved her unconditionally.

The month at Balmoral, which concluded the honeymoon, proved simply torturous to Diana. She had spent time previously with the royal family, but not for such a long period. The 20-year-old princess was bored stiff listening to endless stories from elderly relations during dinner, or hearing Princess Margaret perform ancient show tunes on the piano, or being sent out of the room so the men could enjoy conversation and cigars. And as difficult as it was for Diana to adapt to life in the royal family, her behavior was equally perplexing to them. They wrongly believed that she was practiced in the social graces. Though she wasn't raised in royalty, she was brought up in aristocracy, after all. But they didn't understand that the only lessons Diana received in such matters were in school. Johnnie Spencer was certainly not one to cultivate proper manners; he didn't even eat dinner with his offspring. And the children either avoided Raine's stuffy parties or were encouraged not to attend.

During the month at Balmoral, Diana often left the dinner table early with no explanation or refused to come down for meals at all, which in the traditional and staid world of British royalty was considered quite disrespectful. Such perceived defiance in the presence of the queen was both baffling and unacceptable. Yet baffling and unacceptable could have also described Charles's early reaction to married life. It took him all of two days on the *Brittania* to call Camilla and ask her for advice. "The Prince simply had to be in constant contact with Camilla or he couldn't function properly," said valet Stephen Barry. "If he went without his daily phone call he would become tetchy and ill-tempered."[5]

It didn't help that Diana begged him to take her back to London. She had spoken a year earlier about how Balmoral was her favorite spot in the world. She had told an interviewer after the engagement was announced that the love of the country was one aspect of life she and the prince had in common. Now she was describing it as wet and boring. Charles attempted to explain to her that the royal family was currently at Balmoral and that her job now was to be with them.

A LACK OF CHEMISTRY

Diana had saved herself for marriage with the notion of waiting for that special moment with a special man, but her experiences with Charles during the honeymoon proved disappointing. The feeling was mutual. Perhaps Diana's anticipation of a first sexual encounter exceeded reality. But the letdown on their wedding night played a significant role in the lack of passion they showed for each other throughout the honeymoon. "I had read all that stuff about being swept away and the earth moving, but it wasn't like that at all," Diana recalled. "It was all over in a moment. I just lay there thinking to myself, 'Is that it? Is this really the big deal everybody makes it out to be?' (All he wanted to do was) jump my bones. [His technique was] roll on, roll off, go to sleep."[6] Prince Charles was also disappointed, telling friends that her inexperience left him lacking and that her bulimic purging proved to be a turn-off. The result was that Charles and Diana rarely made love on their honeymoon.

By October, the relationship had reached such an ebb that Charles summoned aide Michael Colborne to come to Balmoral and take care of Diana for a while. Diana had actually requested Colborne, who had been quite supportive of her during the engagement. When Colborne arrived, he was stunned to see how thin she had become. And instead of staying with her for a couple of hours at a time, he found himself watching her sitting in silent agony or listening to her tirades for three times that long. She tearfully moaned to Colborne that she had reached the end of her rope. That was one sentiment about which she and Charles agreed—and once again Colborne was stuck in the middle. Colborne overheard the couple arguing heatedly on several occasions, including one in which he arrived in the room just in time to catch Diana's wedding ring, tossed to him by Charles. Charles told Colborne to get the ring made smaller in a snide reference to Diana's shrinking body.

It appeared that the prince also needed Colborne as a sounding board and adviser. Charles spoke to him about Diana's possessiveness and what he perceived as her rejection of country life. What he didn't mention was her jealousy of Camilla. Many friends and royal family members believe Diana's obsession with Camilla eventually drove the prince into her arms. Others offer that any newlywed would have been angered had her husband remained in constant contact with the woman who had been his mistress. Diana understood instinctively that his feelings for Camilla would always prevent him from loving her unconditionally.

Shortly thereafter, Diana was granted her wish to be taken to London, but not for the reasons she had hoped. Charles and the queen decided she needed professional help, so they sent Diana to a psychoanalyst. The royal family had always shunned such steps and had believed since the honeymoon began that Diana was merely experiencing postwedding jitters, so the hiring of a professional indicated tremendous concern. Diana later reported that she saw several therapists and pharmacologists who prescribed high-powered drugs she refused to take. In addition, she withheld medical information such as her bouts with bulimia that would have been critical to any treatment plan. Whether she was simply being stubborn or her view had validity, Diana believed that she was the same woman she had always been and that she would eventually become used to her life as part of the royal family. She recalled what she perceived to be an endless string of analysts and psychiatrists attempting to figure out what made her tick and trying to prescribe Valium and other drugs, when she believed all she needed was time and patience. Diana felt the professionals remained content prescribing pills simply because they hoped to avoid a violent episode.

The honeymoon ended mercifully in mid-October. The couple was forced to move into Charles's old place in Buckingham Palace since neither Highgrove nor their Kensington Palace homes were prepared for them. Charles and Diana were off to a difficult start.

Actually, one scenario could have made matters worse—if Diana had become pregnant with a child neither she nor Charles wanted. So when she learned she was indeed pregnant as the honeymoon wound down, disaster could have followed. But it had quite the opposite effect, at least temporarily. Preparation for motherhood gave her an opportunity to occupy both her mind and her time. The prince was equally optimistic that the pregnancy would stabilize his wife.

THE PEOPLE'S CHOICE

Later that month, the couple visited Wales, their own principality. Though Diana did not look well, her ability to relate to others shone through. She displayed a love for the people, who showed the same affection in return. Freelance photographer Jayne Fincher recalls her reaching deep into the crowd to touch people rather than resorting to the gentle royal handshake. She contrasted Diana's outgoing and personal style with the queen's quite dignified, formal approach to commoners. Fincher recalled the queen accepting flowers in an elegant manner with her white-gloved hand outstretched. Diana, on the other hand, didn't wear gloves, and she reached enthusiastically for flowers.

Those who believed "Dianamania" would die down after the wedding were badly mistaken. Crowds besieging her during public appearances proved equally large and enthusiastic. And that caused a problem for Charles, who was being overshadowed. On one occasion during the trip to Wales, he decided to greet the people on the opposite side of the road, so he switched sides with Diana. The disappointed moan from those who had clamored to see Diana on that side of the street was loud and embarrassing to Charles. At first he accepted the crowd's desires and collected

flowers for his wife with a smile on his face. But as it became more apparent that the people had only come to see her, he became angered. "She's
over there!" he would bark when the crowd called to see Diana. "Do you
want your money back?"[7] Charles told a Buckingham Palace official that
people didn't care to see him. He asked himself why. He was, after all,
the *Prince of Wales*. When Diana rested, Charles would make speeches
in other parts of the principality, and the press coverage was virtually
nonexistent.

Diana was sympathetic to the plight of her husband. She asked those in
charge of such events if crowds on Prince Charles's side of the road could
be increased in numbers, but one can't sway the passions of a people. Diana
understood the prince's ego had been severely bruised, but she saw no way
around it. Wales was his territory. Its Caernarvon Castle was the site of
his Coming of Age ceremony 12 years earlier, which had been televised
with great interest throughout the nation. Now a woman unknown just a
year earlier was upstaging him. "If you're a man, like my husband a proud
man, you mind about that if you hear it every day for four weeks," Diana
told British Broadcasting Corporation interviewer Martin Bashir years
later about the perceived shift of power in the relationship. "And you feel
low about it, instead of feeling happy and sharing it."[8] The royal family
was feeling pretty low about it as well. Diana had hoped to hear words of
praise for her popularity and performance in Wales, but she received only
silence. Some believe this was because the royal family simply considered
it to be doing her duty. She told longtime friend James Colthurst that she
received an angry response from Charles after the tour.

Soon the queen would get a taste of Dianamania, which found its way
into the State Opening of Parliament on November 4, 1981. The annual event is intended to provide a spotlight moment for Her Majesty.
She is photographed sitting on a throne in the House of Lords donning
the Imperial State Crown, which features the glistening Black Prince's
ruby. The ceremony features a great deal of fanfare, including the blaring
of trumpets. Members of the House of Commons listen intently to the
queen's speech. The occasion serves as a reminder that even though the
queen holds little power in this day and age, she remains an important
figure. Yet she wasn't the most beloved figure on that day or on any other
State Opening of Parliament over the next decade. That distinction belonged to Diana, who took over the show through no desire of her own.
Most everyone in attendance focused on Diana as she emerged from the
glass coach that had whisked her from Westminster to the House of Lords.
The crowds also wondered what she would be wearing, as she had dressed
quite scantily during a previous event to divert Charles's attention from

Camilla. On this occasion, she wore a simple white chiffon gown with a tiara and pearl choker. Her youth and beauty stole attention away from 55-year-old Queen Elizabeth II.

So did a photo taken that evening of Diana fast asleep on the red velvet throne that the Victoria and Albert Museum provided for her so she could sit next to Prince Charles. The picture appeared in newspapers throughout the world the next day and was interpreted not as one of a bored princess, but rather of a tired one. The news of her pregnancy was soon revealed. Stepgrandmother Barbara Cartland broke the story to the *Daily Express*. "The first baby should be conceived in the full bloom of romance!" she crowed. "This baby will be a victory over the horrid modern practice of putting off a family until one or both partners' careers are established. It is a great mistake to delay a first child. It is interfering with nature and nature always knows best. I hope it will be a son because it's what every English man and woman wants."[9]

Full bloom of romance, indeed! The child was conceived during a quite less than passionate honeymoon by a couple whose deep love for each other had proved quite questionable. Nevertheless, Diana was now physically ill, emotionally drained, unhappily wed, and expecting a child. It was a combination that would lead to further unrest between her and Prince Charles, as well as a more severe depression for the princess.

NOTES

1. Tim Clayton and Phil Craig, *Diana: Story of a Princess* (New York: Simon and Schuster, 2001), 83.

2. Sarah Bradford, *Diana* (New York: Viking Press, 2006), 92.

3. Sally Bedell Smith, *Diana in Search of Herself* (New York: Times Books, 1999), 116.

4. Tina Brown, *The Diana Chronicles* (New York: Doubleday, 2007), 175.

5. Ibid., 174.

6. Simone Simmons, *Diana: The Last Word* (New York: St. Martin's Press, 2005), 30.

7. Jay Mulvaney, *Diana and Jackie* (New York: St. Martin's Press, 2002), 193.

8. Diana, Princess of Wales, interview by Martin Bashir, *Panorama*, BBC, November 20, 1995 (citations from BBC transcript).

9. Ralph G. Martin, *Charles & Diana* (Boston: G.K. Hall, 1986), 243.

Chapter 7

EARLY YEARS AS A ROYAL

Though whisperings of a less-than-idyllic relationship between Charles and Diana occasionally appeared in media reports, most believed that the page had been turned from the fairy tale wedding to a marriage destined for a happy ending.

That couldn't have been further from the truth. Upon returning to London at the end of October, the couple moved into a tiny apartment in an upper floor of Buckingham Palace consisting of a bedroom, sitting room, bathroom, and two dressing rooms; it didn't even have a kitchen. Diana couldn't make a cup of coffee or small breakfast or lunch for herself. Charles gave the inconveniences little thought. He had grown up in Buckingham Palace and was accustomed to having everything done for him down to the last detail, including the preparation of meals. But Diana enjoyed the occasional domestic chore. It made her feel useful.

What she did feel was lonely. While the prince traveled about in his official capacity, she had no official capacity. She would phone friends simply to hear a familiar voice. She would accompany her husband to various functions, but she was depressed at the lack of impact she had and the time she spent alone. She still didn't understand why Charles couldn't enjoy more than just a few fleeting moments with her. She wanted to be loved passionately by a husband more devoted to her than to his position. It was too much to ask of Prince Charles, but she rightly questioned whether he truly loved her at all.

Pregnancy didn't help her physical, mental, or emotional state. She felt ill every day. It became difficult to distinguish between bulimia and morning sickness. Diana even canceled a visit to Bristol in mid-November because of her sickness, regardless of what she considered her duty as a princess, who, after all, was supposed to show a stiff upper lip.

Much has been discussed about Diana's decision to have a baby so early in her life and marriage. She certainly yearned for ways to occupy her time and wanted to do her part in carrying on the British traditions. After all, a son would be heir to the throne. Diana also believed that the most effective way to develop a positive relationship with Charles and the royal family was to bring a child into their world. Yet one consultant gynecologist at a London hospital offered that Diana's timing at becoming pregnant would prove disastrous for her. "I always tell women that the two things they shouldn't do if they don't want things to go wrong is get themselves exhausted or under too much strain," he was quoted as saying in an article that appeared in *News of the World*. "The Princess is constantly on public view, which we already know creates stress in her because she collapsed in tears at a polo match just before the wedding."[1]

The hounding by the media increased during that stressful period, and Diana was quite self-conscious. She wasn't particularly vain, but she was driven by maintaining a healthy self-image. On one occasion in December, Diana ran a simple errand to a local sweet shop, whereupon she was besieged by photographers who snapped several pictures that appeared in publications the following day. Finally, the royal family intervened. The queen's press secretary, Michael Shea, convoked media members to Buckingham Palace. They were asked to give the princess a little space. Both the queen and the Duke of Edinburgh spoke to them briefly. They reminded reporters that Diana had not been raised in a family accustomed to such coverage and that the intense scrutiny and suffocating daily routine of the media was taking a toll on her. One of the reporters asked why Diana didn't simply send a footman to the sweet shop, to which the queen replied angrily, "Do you know, I think that's the most pompous remark I've heard in my life."[2]

The long-awaited show of support aside, the pleas were largely ignored by media members, who were not given to succumbing to the urgings of the royal family nor about to follow the rules of others. Though the incessant tabloid coverage of Diana slowed a bit for a brief time, the overzealous treatment of her by the respected media, but particularly by the tabloid media, was to remain a constant source of frustration and despair for the princess for the rest of her life.

Diana did receive a brief respite from her misery during the holiday season in 1981. She managed to escape with Charles to Windsor, where she felt far more relaxed and cheerful. He gave her an emerald-and-diamond ring, which she admitted mesmerized her. Charles wrote to a friend of their happy times in celebrating their first Christmas together.

He was hopeful that the 1982 holiday season would prove even jollier with a newborn baby to share.

HITTING ROCK BOTTOM

The glad tidings from the holiday season were only temporary. Diana's misery returned after the New Year. The couple was visiting Sandringham, where Charles spent much of his time hunting, an activity that Diana despised. Her emotional state became so distressful that she contemplated suicide. It reached such a horrific level in January that she threw herself down the stairs. She claimed it was not an attempt to end her life, but one to dramatize her feelings of helplessness. "Charles said I was crying wolf," recalled Diana, "and I said I felt so desperate and I was crying my eyes out and he said, 'I'm not going to listen. You're always doing this to me. I'm going riding now.' So I threw myself down the stairs. The Queen comes out, absolutely horrified, shaking—she was so frightened. I knew I wasn't going to lose the baby, quite bruised round the stomach. Charles went out riding and when he came back, you know, it was just dismissed, total dismissal."[3] Reports of the incident were sketchy. Others have claimed Diana told a staff member that she merely tripped and fell down the stairs and was shocked to discover that the queen had witnessed it. Published accounts claim that Charles even called a doctor, whose examination revealed no injury to Diana or the baby. But in either case, Diana's feeling of desperation at the time can't be disputed.

Diana received reactions to her bouts of depression that ranged from sympathy and anger toward Charles for the perceived ill treatment of his wife to a critical cry for her to buck up and get herself together for the sake of herself, the royal family, and her baby. Some considered her cries for help to be merely self-pity. After all, from the outside looking in, being married to the Prince of Wales, whiling away your time at such historic sites as Buckingham Palace, and being waited on hand and foot do not qualify in the minds of most as miserable experiences. Yet Diana couldn't shake it. Her unhappiness intensified as her pregnancy went on. In early 1982, she and Charles embarked on a trip to Windermere Island in the Bahamas for what was considered to be a second honeymoon. Diana only wished it could have been done in secret, for the British tabloid press was out in full force. They snapped pictures of Diana, five months pregnant, in a bikini—the tabloids had added sexuality to their list of reasons for their interest in her. One headline in the *Sun* screamed: "carefree Di threw royal caution to the winds to wear her revealing outfit." She couldn't even find privacy on a remote spot 3,000 miles away from home.[4]

The photos angered both the queen and Diana. The latter had always been overwhelmed by the media attention, but had previously understood the necessities of their work to some degree. The pictures of her running around the Bahamas in a bikini proved to be the turning point in her relationship with the tabloid press. She saw no reason for her privacy to be invaded to such an extent.

She discovered another problem in the Bahamas. The couple was staying with Penny and Norton Romsey, close friends of Charles's with whom he had discussed his and Diana's marital difficulties. They were among the most outspoken of those attempting to convince Diana to stop what they perceived to be her self-pity. Though she enjoyed herself in the Bahamas and had finally been afforded time alone with Charles, she reacted angrily when he went off by himself to read or paint and even openly complained of being bored. Diana was also suspicious that her husband had taken her to the Bahamas not for a second honeymoon, but so his friends could prey on her.

She was further taxed by "The Diana Watch" in the media, which speculated daily as to when the future king would be born. She decided to have her labor induced, against the advice of her gynecologist, George Pinker, who preferred a more natural approach. Diana gave birth sooner than expected, but the labor itself was a slow and painful process. It took 16 hours, during which time a cesarean section was discussed and Diana had an epidural injection to relieve the pain. But at 9:03 pm on June 21, 1982, William was born and a nation celebrated. Diana had produced an heir to the throne, a firstborn son for Prince Charles, and a grandson for the queen.

Her eating disorder temporarily subsided due to her enthusiasm about motherhood. Friend Carolyn Bartholomew, who visited Diana at Kensington Palace three days after the birth of William, marveled at how excited Diana was about herself and her baby. Bartholomew saw a contentment in Diana she hadn't witnessed in quite a while. Diana herself felt the same way. "It was a great relief because it was all peaceful again," Diana remembered years later. "And I was well for a time."[5] So was Charles, who spoke glowingly to the media and to family members about the experience of becoming a father. He had remained by Diana's side throughout the difficult labor. Though only a temporary salvation to their marital problems, having a baby together allowed them to forge a bond. "The arrival of our small son has been an astonishing experience and one that has meant more to me than could ever have imagined," Charles wrote in a letter to godmother Patricia Mountbatten. "I am SO thankful I was beside Diana's bedside the whole time because I really felt as though I'd shared deeply in the process of birth and as a result was rewarded by seeing a small creature which belonged to US even though he seemed to belong to everyone else as well."[6]

After the birth of William, the new parents moved into their London home of Kensington Palace, which was finally ready. The weeks that followed were among the happiest of Diana's life as Princess of Wales. Princess Margaret threw a high-spirited reception for the couple. Diana was satisfied that she had fulfilled her obligation to the crown. Soon, however, she not only felt the effects of postpartum depression, but she began experiencing panic attacks when Charles was late returning home. She felt a strong sense of abandonment. Outsiders might have believed that she should have been celebrating her 21st birthday in July with a sense of joy because her life seemed complete, but the aftereffects of childbirth worsened her mood.

Diana's behavior, even by her own admission, became unpredictable. The bulimia affected her mood, but she was also beginning to experience insomnia. During the annual royal family vacation at Balmoral, she went sleepless for three nights while continuing to binge and purge. Her weight dropped frighteningly. Disagreement remains as to whether the royal family was aware of her eating disorder.

HER AGAIN

Then, as always, there was Camilla. On one occasion, Diana eavesdropped on her husband while he was on the phone with his longtime friend. Diana overheard Charles say, "Whatever happens, I will always love you."[7] Charles claimed to biographer Jonathan Dimbleby that upon his engagement he had very little contact with Camilla for the next five years. The lone exceptions were at various social functions. He added that he spoke to Camilla just once during his marriage and only to inform her that Diana was pregnant. Charles told Dimbleby that he never spoke with Camilla after the birth of William until he resumed his relationship with her in 1986. Those who have reported that Charles often saw Camilla during fox hunting excursions dispute such an assertion. Others have offered that the press saw Charles and Camilla riding side by side during an event shortly after the trip to Wales, but didn't print the story because the fairy tale factor of the royal marriage was still fresh in the minds of the public. Whatever the reality of Charles's relationship with Camilla during the early years of his marriage, it can't be doubted that it weighed heavily upon the fears of Diana.

Coupled with the enormity of her position as Princess of Wales, her suspicions of Charles led to her depression. But the prince, arguably

overthinking the problem, believed intense psychoanalysis was the answer. He summoned mentor Laurens van der Post, whose books he had
devoured on the honeymoon. The 80-year-old van der Post was a fascinating man, having survived a Japanese prisoner-of-war camp during
World War II and having lived with the Kalahari Bushmen of Africa.
But his ability to identify with 21-year-old Diana was questionable at
best. He recommended that Diana visit London psychiatrist Dr. Alan
McGlashan. Diana complained that not only was Dr. McGlashan nearly
as old as van der Post, but he was far too interested in analyzing her
dreams. But because Diana felt that she had been fine before she became
engaged to Charles, she decided to seek out Dr. David Mitchell. She
spoke with him on a nightly basis at Kensington Palace. Mitchell explored her relationship with Charles, which in her mind was a huge part
of the problem, along with the loss of the carefree existence she enjoyed
as a more typical young woman in London. But she failed to give Mitchell or any professional analyst details of her bulimia, which had certainly
affected her state of mind since the wedding.

Somehow, Diana was able to hide her distress in public. One such example occurred late in September 1982 when she traveled to Monaco for
the funeral of Princess Grace, who died from injuries suffered in a car accident—a spooky precursor to Diana's own tragic end. The event was tailor-
made for Diana. Monaco is known as a mecca of elegance and glamour,
which certainly fit her description, and this was an occasion that required
tact and sympathy, both of which she had in abundance. Diana was well
received in Monaco and was praised for her performance. But reminiscent
of her experience when she stole the show in Wales, she wasn't about to
extract even the slightest positive response from the royal family.

"Look at the papers," an aide told her the day after she returned from
Monaco. "They say you did brilliantly."

"Good," she answered. "Because nobody mentioned it here."[8]

The royal family didn't believe it should have been mentioned. In its
eyes, neither Princess Diana nor any of its other members are performers.
They represent Great Britain and the royal family on official visits such
as the one in Monaco, and they are not to be congratulated for doing
their jobs. And therein lay the problem. Diana had barely completed her
teenage years and was painfully sensitive at the time. She yearned to be
appreciated by Charles and the royal family, but such appreciation was
not forthcoming.

The frenzied reaction to Diana carried with it another negative con-
sequence to her marriage through no fault of her own—it made Charles
jealous. Playing second fiddle to Diana was not what he had in mind when

he married her. On a trip to Australia and New Zealand in March 1983, *Daily Mirror* photographer Kent Gavin reported that out of every 100 photos snapped by the nearly 200 photographers present, 92 focused on Diana. The throngs besieging her were incredible. An estimated 300,000 individuals crowded the streets of Brisbane. The same hysteria followed her to the Australian capital city of Sydney. Just as in Wales, folks expressed disappointment when Charles rather than Diana greeted them. He expressed a curiosity about her appeal in a letter he wrote to a friend in early April while he and Diana were in Australia. "Maybe the wedding, because it was so well done, and because it made such a wonderful, almost Hollywood-style film, has distorted people's view of things?" he asked.[9]

BLOSSOMING PRINCESS

Such fervent support by the common person everywhere she went, coupled by the painful silence from the royal family, changed Diana in a profound way. She realized that her real gift and her real love was relating to people. She not only had a knack for interacting with the masses, but felt a genuine empathy with them. Her need to take care of those less fortunate had been transformed from the furry animals for which she cared as a child to the people of the world. The reaction she received served to alter her view of Charles. She was taken aback by what she viewed as his jealousy. That realization made her stronger and increased her self-confidence. Perhaps she was above it all. Despite being sick with bulimia and feeling jet-lagged after criss-crossing around the country, Diana couldn't help but feel wonderful about her natural ability to relate to people. It *wasn't* just that she was Charles's wife—it was *her*.

Diana spoke about what she perceived as Charles's jealousy of her to biographer Andrew Morton. She recalled Charles taking his poor showing in Australia out on her. She tried to comfort him by saying that no matter who his wife was, she was bound to receive a great deal of attention as Princess of Wales. Diana expressed her feelings to him that he should be proud of her simply because she was his wife. However, she didn't believe that Charles saw the situation the same way.

Victor Chapman, who served as press secretary on the tour, claimed he received several phone calls from Charles complaining about the lack of media attention he was receiving. Charles wrote to one friend that the incredible press coverage of Diana was bound to have a negative effect on her. After all, how could she emerge from it with the same self-image? He was both right and wrong. Diana did indeed develop an insatiable curiosity about what the media was writing and saying about her. When she returned from Australia, she devoured analyses of her performance in the tabloids and in the more traditional British press. But was that a negative development? Many would argue that it simply served to strengthen her view of herself and gave her a stronger sense of independence and self-worth.

A subsequent three-week excursion to Canada produced the same results. While the media lavished praise on Diana, they largely ignored Charles. One *Ottawa Citizen* article even referred to him as an "also-ran." Words such as that cut him to the quick. He asked one friend, "Why do they love her so much? All she ever did was say 'yes' to me."[10] It was at this time that Michael Colborne decided he'd had enough of being caught in the middle of their squabbles. Charles's longtime personal secretary, whom he had summoned to look after Diana, resigned in December after the prince had accused him of spending too much time with her. Colborne understandably replied that spending time with Diana was what he thought Charles *wanted* him to do, which prompted the prince to fly into a rage. Charles then opened the door to find Diana sobbing as she listened to the tirade. The incident prompted Colborne to call it quits after a decade of service to Charles.

Meanwhile, Diana developed a sense of independence in how she raised William. She steadfastly refused to instill in him what she considered to be the stuffy, self-indulgent attitude of a royal family member. She enrolled William (and later second son Harry) in Wetherby, a rather unpretentious preschool in Notting Hill. Diana also didn't encourage a fawning and revered outlook at the royal family in her sons. When William was little, a classmate asked him if he knew Queen Elizabeth II. "Don't you mean Granny?" he asked.[11]

Diana didn't allow her enormous popularity and calling as a princess to overshadow her duties as a mother. When the royal family disallowed William to be taken on long official visits, as he was to Australia and New Zealand, she responded that she would no longer embark on lengthy trips. She didn't want William to be left in the care of others while she traveled the world. As much as anyone, Diana understood the suffering of children who don't have parents around to keep them emotionally strong. She was, after all, victimized not only by the divorce of her parents, but by the lack of nurturing from them when she was a child. She had learned from the past and was not about to make the same mistakes.

The same held true for her first few years as Princess of Wales. From this point forward, she would display an independence of thought and action that spoke to her growing maturity. Certainly she was upset when she discovered that Charles and Camilla were again more than just friends, but rather than respond like a weak and jealous schoolgirl, she used the strength and confidence gained through success and maturity to become one of the most respected and admired women in the world.

NOTES

1. Fiona MacDonald Hull, Geraldine Hosier, and Sara Rust, *News of the World*, November 15, 1981.

2. Tim Clayton and Phil Craig, *Diana: Story of a Princess* (New York: Simon and Schuster, 2001), 101.

3. Sarah Bradford, *Diana* (New York: Viking Press, 2006), 104.

4. Ibid., 105.

5. Sally Bedell Smith, *Diana in Search of Herself* (New York: Times Books, 1999), 131.

6. Jonathan Dimbleby, *The Prince of Wales: A Biography* (London: Little, Brown and Company, 1993), 304.

7. Smith, *Diana in Search of Herself*, 134.

8. Tina Brown, *The Diana Chronicles* (New York: Doubleday, 2007), 218.

9. Ibid., 220.

10. Bradford, *Diana*, 118.

11. Brown, *The Diana Chronicles*, 223.

Chapter 8

THE CRUMBLING MARRIAGE

The frightened, cowering, jealous Diana was gone by the fall of 1983. Her suspicions of Charles had evolved into certainty, and she was convinced that he had resumed his affair with Camilla. But she stood up to her husband. She still hoped to save her marriage, but at a certain point she understood all was lost. That point was reached on September 15, 1984, when she gave birth to second son Harry. Charles had openly rooted for a girl, which prompted Diana to keep the sex of the child a secret from him. She claimed that when Harry was born, Charles didn't hide his disappointment, even commenting derisively that the child sported red hair, which was a Spencer trait. "Something inside me died," Diana told friends about that moment.[1] It was indeed the beginning of the end for the fairy tale couple.

And though throughout Charles's adult life he displayed an affinity toward strong women, he wasn't taken with his wife's newfound strength. One senior Buckingham Palace official told the story of a marriage on the verge of collapse as the mid-1980s approached, even though it officially lasted several more years. "(Charles) didn't change his bachelor ways," the official said. "She wanted him to stay at home with her and the children. She challenged him—it was the first time he had been challenged. It was the first time he had met his equal—he was surrounded by yes-men."[2]

Though Diana's assertion that Charles was disappointed that she had given birth to another boy has been denied, her love and attention for both William and Harry cannot be. Even those critical of Diana for her behavior during the marriage have marveled at the joy she brought to mothering. The postpartum depression she experienced after William arrived did not return following the birth of Harry. Her life revolved around the boys. She organized parties for them and stuck notes on doors expressing her love for them. She also proved to be a conscientious mother, making them pick up their toys and regulating their intake of sweets. Diana became even closer to William and Harry after her divorce, mostly because her emotional needs had grown, but the love she felt for them was deep from the moment they were born.

Though both Diana and Charles displayed a tremendous affection for their children, they continued to drift apart. It became apparent by the mid-1980s that they were mismatched from the start. Diana had become the fashion darling of Great Britain. Every new dress, every new hairdo, every new piece of jewelry worn by the princess became fodder for the media. Charles and the rest of the royal family were pushed to the inside pages of the newspapers as photos of the glamorous Diana consumed the front. When she wore her hair up for the first time at the 1984 State Opening of Parliament, which is intended to place the spotlight on the queen, Diana's new hairstyle bumped Elizabeth II from the front page. New publications that were to be devoted entirely to the royal family focused almost exclusively on Diana and her children. Diana became increasingly aware of the attention paid to her wardrobe and began traveling with hundreds of different outfits.

While Charles proved far more reflective and introspective, particularly at that point in their lives, Diana was now in her mid-20s and was more in tune with the entertainment world. In July 1985, they attended the famed Live Aid rock concert at Wembley Stadium in London to raise money for starving people in Ethiopia. While Diana could be seen dancing to the music of such legends as Madonna, David Bowie, and former Beatle Paul McCartney, Charles looked downright bored and out of place in his suit and tie.

TWO CAN PLAY AT THIS GAME

Diana, now convinced that her husband had resumed his relationship with Camilla, began showing her flirtatious side as well. Reporter Judy Wade spoke about one occasion in which Diana openly flirted with Andrew Morton, a member of the press corps who later wrote a controversial biography of the princess. The two had an ongoing and whimsical dialogue about his colorful ties. Wade related that during a cocktail party, Diana grabbed Morton's tie and pulled him close to her while the stunned media members looked on. "God, I think I'll have to get a bucket of water and throw it over them," exclaimed one press officer.[3]

By the time Diana and Charles made their much-anticipated trip to the United States, the princess had been cast as the dominant figure in the relationship. An article cleverly titled "The Mouse That Roared" in the October 1985 issue of *Vanity Fair*, written by Tina Brown, who also went on to pen a biography of Diana, proved quite unflattering to both. Brown claimed that the princess had Charles squarely under her thumb. She offered that the rise to stardom had negatively affected Diana and that Charles was cranky, dull, and old beyond his 36 years. She further claimed that Diana was addicted to shopping and reading about herself in the press because she was obsessed with her public image.

The highlight of the U.S. tour was a banquet and ball given by President and Mrs. Reagan, during which Diana enjoyed a notable dance with American actor John Travolta. At an event at the Royal Opera House at Covent Garden two months later, Diana tried to spice up her relationship with Charles by slipping into a slinky white satin dress and dancing seductively for him. The movements were quite against the royal grain, but many of those in attendance were entranced by her startling act. Unfortunately, Charles wasn't one of them. He reacted coolly to what he considered to be an exhibition that flew in the face of royal etiquette. It was obvious he was displeased.

Was the marriage finally over at that point? Though Charles had claimed that he spoke with Camilla only once—to announce Diana's first pregnancy—during a five-year period, and that he returned to Camilla only after the marriage was irretrievably lost, many close to the couple believe the renewal of his physical relationship with Camilla extended back to 1983. Diana lamented that the couple rarely shared the same bed after William was born. Friends of Charles's claim they arranged a reunion between him and Camilla in 1986 because they felt he was miserable and simply needed someone to talk to. Charles had always believed that Camilla was a wonderful confidante. She too was in an unhappy marriage at the time, which prompted friends, particularly the same Patti Palmer-Tomkinson who had been won over by Diana before the wedding, to get them back together. Soon phone calls turned into dates, and dates turned into intimate encounters. According to Charles, that wasn't what he had in mind at all when he resumed his relationship with Camilla. But he was at his wit's end. "Frequently I feel nowadays that I'm in a kind of cage, pacing up and down in it and longing to be free," he wrote to a friend in late 1986. "How awful incompatibility is, and how dreadfully destructive it can be. . . . I fear I'm going to need a bit of help every now and then for which I feel rather ashamed."[4]

Though physical proof has never existed that Charles had resumed his affair with Camilla between the births of William and Harry, the hunting expeditions together and the time away from home indicate that his claim that they spoke only once by phone until 1986 was inaccurate. Diana found Charles on the phone with Camilla on more than one occasion, which raised suspicions. He remained silent whenever Diana brought up her concerns about his relationship with Camilla. When Diana had convinced herself that they were indeed together again, she felt betrayed. She began referring to Camilla as "the Rottweiler" because "she looks like a dog—and because once she has got her teeth into someone she won't let go."[5]

Many believe Diana didn't want to let go of Barry Mannakee, a personal protection officer with whom she grew quite close in the mid-1980s. Though she had emerged from her shell by that time, she remained emotionally needy, especially since she was convinced that Charles had resumed sexual relations with Camilla. Mannakee provided Diana with the comfort and praise she so desperately craved. She fell into his arms often when distraught and tearful. The relationship became quite friendly and flirtatious. She referred to him as "my fella" and playfully ran her hands over her evening gown and asked him with a sexy tone, "Do I look all right?" He would reply, "I could quite fancy you myself," whereupon she would purr, "But you do already, don't you?"[6]

Such exchanges were bound to make the rounds. Senior protection officer Colin Trimming warned Mannakee that he was getting too close to Diana. Mannakee was removed from his position in 1986 and died tragically in a motorcycle accident the following year. Diana suspected foul play, but she later learned that a young automobile driver seeking her license had killed him by accident. Diana considered Mannakee her best friend, someone in whom she could confide. She thought of him as a father or an older brother and insisted they never had sex, though a decade later she told Charles's biographer Anthony Holden that Mannakee, who had a wife and two kids, had been the love of her life. Charles had become aware of his wife's relationship with Mannakee, but believed it to be nonsexual. Even if he had suspicions, he claimed it had nothing to do with his decision to renew his affair with Camilla.

NEW GIRL IN TOWN

Camilla wasn't the only competition for Diana. In the summer of 1986, Sarah Ferguson wed Prince Andrew at Westminster Abbey and became the Duchess of York. A year older than Diana, she was also more bubbly and worldly. She assumed her role without a hitch, at least for a while, and the royal family embraced her immediately. At her first trip to Balmoral, an annual holiday that Diana dreaded, "Fergie" showed a great deal of spirit in spending time with the queen, the Queen Mother, and the Duke of Edinburgh. Diana could be overheard by Mrs. Danvers of the Highgrove staff screaming her objections at the prospect of another trip to the castle she so hated. Fergie, on the other hand, spoke with passion about "the perfect haven, a staunch fortress against the arrows . . . I loved the crackle of its morning frost and the smells of the heather and peaty soil, so delicious and earthy."[7]

While Diana was still seen almost as a stranger by the royal family, Fergie fit in right away. Not only did Charles take notice, but he was also quick to point out the differences to his wife, asking her point-blank why she couldn't be more like the Duchess of York. Diana was not threatened or angered by Fergie's presence. On the contrary, the inclusion of Fergie into the royal family gave her someone her own age to relate to. Diana had known her for several years. And despite the fact that Fergie blended in with the royal family with far more desire and success, she admired Diana and thoroughly enjoyed her company. Diana, on the other hand, didn't mind Sarah stealing the media spotlight for a while. Let her every move be analyzed and reanalyzed, figured the Princess of Wales. And, simply put, she had more fun with Fergie than she'd had with anyone since her carefree days at Coleherne Court. The two dressed as policewomen in an unsuccessful attempt to crash Andrew's bachelor party. They were arrested and tossed into a police van before they were recognized and released. They proceeded to a nearby nightclub, where they drank champagne and acted silly. It was the kind of mindless fun Diana had been yearning for since she tied the knot.

And Fergie was fun. At a party she and Andrew hosted to thank those who organized their wedding, she not only encouraged Diana to dance the can-can with her, but also attempted to persuade the guests to jump into the swimming pool fully clothed. On one occasion in June 1987, she and Fergie were photographed poking a courtier on the behind with an umbrella. The stunt was universally panned as childish, and critics claimed that such tomfoolery added to Charles's disenchantment with his wife. Diana, however, was simply enjoying herself. Both she and Fergie derided the stuffiness of royal family etiquette as the years progressed.

Yet Diana felt slighted over the reaction of the royal family to Fergie, who in Diana's mind had been welcomed with open arms for what she was while Diana was ignored for what she did. Fergie's ability to fit in with the royal family earned praise and respect. Diana's personality and performance, which attracted millions to her side throughout the world, brought nothing but silence. The differences in reaction increased the distance between Diana and the royal family. An already impersonal, cold relationship grew even chillier. But the fact that Diana was pained by Fergie's acceptance by the royal family indicated that she still cared about their feelings toward her.

She might not have lost her feelings for Charles at that time, but she certainly believed strongly that her husband was back with Camilla. That's when she began her romantic involvement with Major James Hewitt. Her beauty so struck him that he hoped for an introduction during a party at the St. James Palace apartment of lady-in-waiting Hazel West. Fortunate to have been granted an invitation, he struck up a conversation with Diana about horseback riding. He was an expert rider as staff captain of the Household Division and head of the Household Division stables. She spoke to him of her yearning to conquer her fears of horseback riding, fears she'd had ever since falling off a horse as a child. She phoned him several days later and set up lessons near Kensington Palace. It has been speculated that Diana was more motivated by her physical attraction to Hewitt than by her desire to ride, though Hewitt, an experienced instructor, claimed they both thoroughly enjoyed the lessons. They certainly broke up her rather dull daily routine. The rejection she felt from Charles was as much sexual as anything else, and she was ready to send the same message back to him. It might not have been Diana's first affair, but it was her first admitted one.

Hewitt recalled one lesson that took place following a promotion to acting major that stationed him in Windsor. He was thrilled that Diana wanted to continue her lessons there despite the added travel. But he soon found out that she had more in mind when she said she wanted to be alone with him. He remembered a dinner invitation one evening as the first in which he spent the night. What followed was a full-blown romantic relationship, complete with love poems, hand holding, and secret meetings. In a 1995 magazine interview, Diana admitted to having quickly fallen in love with Hewitt, who shared those same feelings for her. They told each other of that love quite often, which made both feel desired. It was exactly what Diana needed emotionally. Considering how infrequent her sexual encounters with Charles were, she remained quite inexperienced in bed before her affair with Hewitt. But he was enthralled with their love life, risky as it was, as they bounced secretly from Kensington Palace to Highgrove to his mother's home in Devon to avoid detection. "She was utterly charming and natural and fresh and vivacious and rather lovely," praised Hewitt. "There was a certain chemistry right away. . . . She was a woman badly damaged by rejection. Whether it was true or not, she saw herself as being wholly alone in a hostile world."[8]

Shortly before their first sexual interlude, Diana began opening up to him. She spoke about being unloved by Charles, about how the queen didn't appreciate her performance as Princess of Wales, about how she wished her marriage to Charles had turned out differently, and about her belief that the royal family was jealous because of her popularity in comparison to that of her husband. Diana's vulnerabilities became apparent to Hewitt. She even confessed to him her bulimia, a subject she avoided even with the stream of psychoanalysts she had seen. She claimed she didn't experience it when she was with him, but he admitted to being disgusted by it and noticing that he could feel its effects in her skin and its lack of firmness. But in the time he spent with her, often up to two days at a time, Hewitt never saw her binge and purge.

Such a relationship was impossible to hide from everyone. The Royal Protection Squad officers became aware of it, and so did Queen Elizabeth II, who was informed by none other than Diana. The princess gathered up the courage to tell her with the idea that she was the only person who could help. She complained about Charles's infidelity to the queen, who replied that she didn't feel it was her place to get involved. Diana later said that the queen professed helplessness over the situation. "I don't know what you should do," the queen said. "Charles is hopeless."[9]

That perceived hopelessness and lack of affection she was receiving from Charles continued to prey on Diana's self-esteem. Her time with Hewitt provided some of the only moments of joy in her life. Despite the fact that much of the media still bought into the fairy tale marriage, which had been pure nonsense since the honeymoon, it was apparent the relationship was in shambles by 1987. A picture of discontent was drawn during a June wedding reception in which Diana danced seductively with handsome banker Philip Dunne and Charles spent much of the night with old girlfriend Anna Wallace before romantically dancing with Camilla. He finally asked Diana to leave at 2:00 AM, but Diana reportedly laughed in his face and continued to party. She was closing in on her late twenties, sexually satisfied for the first time in her life, and developing into quite the social butterfly.

Though friends and family could detect a problem in the marriage or even knew of affairs involving Charles or Diana, the media had a more difficult time picking up on it because their public relationship remained effective. In fact, during a 1988 official visit to Australia to celebrate its bicentennial, they played the role of loving spouses to the cameras. Diana had decided to go along for the ride as the Princess of Wales, and Charles continued to keep up the public perception of a happy husband, all of which allowed the marriage to survive, at least legally, for quite some time.

But the corner had long been turned toward a marriage of convenience and eventual divorce. The two spent much of their time apart, generally coming together only for official appearances.

As for Diana and Hewitt, that love affair wasn't destined for longevity either. In the end, she was forced to admit that "his head was inside his trousers" and that "he was about as interesting as a knitting pattern."[10] Critics of that relationship believed that they were using each other and that neither was ever truly in love, though both have made attempts to dispel that notion. Some considered Hewitt the right man at the right time for fulfilling Diana's sexual and emotional needs, while Diana gave Hewitt the red carpet to the high life. Hewitt visited Diana often and even became close to William and Harry, reading them bedtime stories and playing with them at the Highgrove home.

Butler Paul Burrell often felt caught in the middle of the respective love affairs of Diana and Charles. Burrell recalled a secretive request from Diana to pick up Hewitt and drive him to see her, whereupon the two embarked on a fervent embrace. But he noted that his experiences dealing with Charles's relationship with Camilla occurred earlier than that of Diana and Hewitt. "It needs to be stressed here that Major James Hewitt was a visitor to Highgrove long after Camilla Parker Bowles," Burrell wrote. "Prince Charles had struck the first blow in that regard. The princess merely rose to equal her husband's level of deceit."[11]

Eventually, however, the shallowness of that relationship was realized. Diana didn't consider Hewitt to be particularly bright. She was growing intellectually and in her awareness of the world around her. Some had begun seeing her as a party girl to whom socializing had become her foremost priority aside from her sons. But by the late 1980s, the woman who as a child and teenager showed so much empathy for those less fortunate was again showing those traits. Such a deep caring for others defined her life until its tragic end.

NOTES

1. Andrew Morton, *Diana: Her True Story* (New York: Simon and Schuster, 1997), 147.

2. Tim Clayton and Phil Craig, *Diana: Story of a Princess* (New York: Simon and Schuster, 2001), 125.

3. Ibid., 133.

4. Penny Junor, *The Firm, The Troubled Life of the House of Windsor* (New York: St. Martin's Press, 2005), 84.

5. Simone Simmons, *Diana: The Last Word* (New York: St. Martin's Press, 2005), 38.

6. Ibid., 46.

7. Tina Brown, *The Diana Chronicles* (New York: Doubleday, 2007), 266.

8. Sarah Bradford, *Diana* (New York: Viking Press, 2006), 157–58.

9. Ibid., 158.

10. Simmons, *Diana: The Last Word,* 50.

11. Paul Burrell, *A Royal Duty* (New York: G. P. Putnam's Sons, 2003), 127.

Princess Diana, early 1990s. Photofest Inc.

Prince Charles, Baby William, Princess Diana, circa 1983. Photofest Inc.

Prince Charles of England and his bride, Princess Diana, July 29, 1981. Photofest Inc.

Prince Charles, Princess Diana, mid 1980s. Photofest Inc.

Princess Diana, 1983. Photofest Inc.

Shown from left: Queen Elizabeth II; Charles, Prince of Wales; Baby William (Prince William Arthur Philip Louis of Wales); Diana, Princess of Wales; Prince Philip; Queen Elizabeth The Queen Mother. Occasion is the christening of William (it is also the Queen Mother's 82nd birthday), August 4, 1982. Photofest Inc.

Lady Diana Spencer, age 19, November 1980. Photofest Inc.

Princess Diana with Princess Anne in the background, on their way to the State Opening of Parliament, November 1981. Photofest Inc.

Young Diana with brother Charles. Central Press/Hulton Archive/Getty Images.

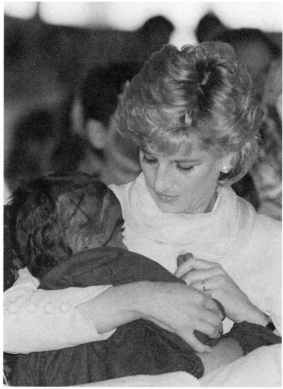

Diana with Pakistani child in Lahore, Pakistan, April 1996. Anwar Hussein/WireImage/Getty Images.

Chapter 9

GROWING COMPASSION

The 1980s were the decade of the Great Divide both in Great Britain and in the United States. The gap between the rich and the poor widened significantly. And though Diana had come from aristocracy and now lived as royalty, both of which obviously benefited from policies catering to the wealthy, the plight of those who suffered brought out her natural compassion. The difference was that now she boasted the fame and influence to make a difference. When money had to be raised, her mere presence at a charitable event would get the funds rolling in.

Diana didn't have to change herself to change the world. In fact, her growing involvement in social causes allowed her to temporarily forget about her personal problems. But in the spring of 1988, an encounter with old friend Carolyn Bartholomew forced her to face her bulimia. Bartholomew, who cared enough about Diana to be angry with her for allowing the disease to fester as long as it did, threatened to inform the media of her illness if she didn't take immediate steps to rid herself of it. The confrontation hit Diana right between the eyes. She knew she had to do something, not only because of the threat of reporters splashing the news all over the front pages of newspapers worldwide, but also because such words coming from one of her best friends jolted her back to reality.

Diana's next step was a phone call to Dr. Maurice Lipsedge, who specialized in eating disorders at Guy's Hospital in Central London and had worked with her sister Sarah in the late 1970s. Diana was stunned when he asked her how many times she had attempted suicide, to which she answered four or five times. Lipsedge continued to pepper pointed questions at her before claiming he could cure her within six months if she could keep her food down. He also offered that the root of her problem was her husband and that she should read books about her condition to better understand it. The immediate success of the treatments has been debated. According to biographer Andrew Morton, Diana's bouts with bulimia slipped from four or five times a week to once every three weeks despite Charles's sarcastic remarks and lack of confidence in the treatments, but they increased drastically whenever she stayed with the royal family at Balmoral, Sandringham, or Windsor.[1] They also worsened when she spent considerable time with Charles at Highgrove, which she claimed to Morton to still detest.

Whatever the case, her attempt to overcome bulimia coincided with her decision to confront the woman of her nightmares—Camilla Parker Bowles. It occurred on the night she and Charles attended the 40th birthday party of Camilla's sister Annabel Elliott. Since Diana and Charles had been spending so little time with each other, the guests assumed that Diana wouldn't show up. And she might not have, had she not arrived with a purpose in mind. Diana found Camilla with Charles and some other guests downstairs. She asked everyone but Camilla to head upstairs, explaining that she had something important to say to her. Though frightened as she heard a commotion upstairs from those who correctly predicted a showdown, Diana told Camilla that she was aware of her affair with Charles and that she felt as though Camilla and the prince were treating her like an ignorant "idiot."[2]

Diana further reported that Charles angrily lit into her in the car on the way home and that she responded with a long crying jag. She barely slept that night, but the next morning she felt as though a heavy weight had been lifted from her shoulders. Though she claimed to her husband that she simply told Camilla that she still loved him and wanted to be a good wife and mother, her actions after the confrontation with his mistress indicate that she was ready to break free from the past pettiness and jealousies that had prevented her from reaching her potential. She certainly didn't choose fidelity at that moment over a continued sexual relationship with Hewitt and, later, other men.

The relationship with Hewitt was apparently not meant to flourish. Not only did they prove intellectually incompatible, but he was given a two-year assignment as leader of a tank squadron in Germany in late 1989. Great Britain was in a state of high alert due to rebellions in East Germany that some believed would lead to military action by the Soviet Union. Diana was disappointed and wanted to work out an arrangement in which they could still meet at least once a week. She was angered when

Hewitt refused, citing his sense of responsibility. Hewitt could hardly be blamed. Events in East Germany were having a profound effect not only on that nation but in Europe and around the world. East Germans fed up with Communist and dictatorial rule tore down the Berlin Wall and eventually forced their leaders to reunite with West Germany after nearly a half century of separation.

MISSIONS OF THE HEART

Though Diana appeared to take far more interest in her personal life than in the state of world affairs, the same couldn't be said for her sympathy for those who were suffering. In early 1989 she took her first solo tour overseas by visiting the United States. Diana asked to spend most of her time in New York City, but not because of its nightlife. Rather, she requested trips through its poorest, most drug-ravaged ghettos and the dilapidated Harlem Hospital, where she visited eight infants with AIDS who would most likely die before their first birthday.

Diana also befriended officials at Henry Street, which worked with battered women and the homeless and had developed into one of the premier social welfare agencies in the United States. Henry Street became greatly respected for employing those who had been homeless and destitute. But to continue its work, Henry Street needed money. It had been threatened with a loss of funding. Although officials had had negative experiences with celebrities, some of whom just sought attention by lending their name to such a charitable cause, they soon discovered that Diana's compassion and desire to help were sincere. "She was genuinely concerned about the issues," recalled former Urban Family Center director Verona Middleton-Jeter. "She asked a lot of questions about . . . what the battered women were going through. . . . I just didn't expect the sincerity. It wasn't like she was a princess or royalty. . . . She related so easily to the residents. It was natural and warm."[3]

Selflessness and caring for those less fortunate had been traits of Diana's throughout her life. Not only did these traits intensify over the years, but she discovered far more about issues for which to be passionate. Rather than use her fame and wealth to create an idyllic life for herself, she turned that good fortune outward to help others. She knew instinctively as a teenager that she had a mission in life, and originally she believed it to revolve around a future husband. But in her role as princess, she eventually realized it related far more poignantly to bringing kindness to those who had been treated unkindly, to bring help to the helpless, and to bring hope to the hopeless. Moreover, she boasted a natural ability to communicate her feelings to those same people, as well as to those who cared for them.

Among those who witnessed Diana's magic touch was Marjatta van Boeschoten, a one-time lawyer and trustee for Paradise House Association, a learning center for disabled adults. Initially van Boeschoten felt little thrill or anticipation in 1983 when she learned that Diana was to visit. But when she saw Diana with one of her staff members, she was overwhelmed. "There was a radiance and a warmth about her as well as her beauty," van Boeschoten recalled. "One could sense her vulnerability. I noticed how she leaned over and listened so attentively to one of the caregivers, giving her full attention. A year later, the caregiver was still moved by it. It was as if everyone there that morning had been touched by light."[4]

Such a story would have come as no surprise to Patrick Jephson, who joined Diana's staff in 1988 as an equerry before becoming her private secretary. On his first day working with her, Jephson was struck by a moment Diana spent with a dying child. He quickly realized that Diana was genuinely touched by the experience and felt a sincere sympathy for the plight of the youngster. That surprised him a bit, as he had been taken aback by the rather crude humor she had displayed in more private moments, sometimes even at the expense of the people she was visiting. But Jephson soon realized that joking about difficult and painful tasks was her way of coping emotionally. As soon as he witnessed the moments she spent with the dying child, his belief in her complete sincerity was cemented. Her reaction when the girl finally passed away gave it further credence.

"As I watched her at a dying child's bedside, holding the girl's newly cold hand and comforting the stricken parents, she seemed to share their grief," Jephson wrote in his biography of Diana. "Not self-consciously like a stranger, not distantly like a counselor, not even through any special experience or deep insight. Instead it just seemed that a tranquility gathered around her. Into this stillness the weeping mother and heartbroken father poured their sorrow and there, somehow, it was safe. The young woman with the smart suit and soulful eyes had no answers for them, but they felt that somewhere inside she knew at least a part of what they were feeling. That was all the moment needed."[5]

No epidemic tugged at Diana's heartstrings more than AIDS, which was first diagnosed in 1983 and developed into one of the deadliest diseases of the decade. It not only brought slow death to its victims, but often made them social outcasts. Though anyone could be inflicted with the HIV that causes AIDS, the outbreak greatly affected the homosexual community.

Diana had numerous gay acquaintances in the fashion industry and on the palace staff. Among those who died of AIDS was Stephen Barry, who had served as Charles's valet. She felt unthreatened and unburdened around gay men, and she felt tremendous pain as the growing disease threatened her friends.

Ignorance about the HIV has always been widespread, but more so in the 1980s, when the disease was relatively new. Many were afraid to come anywhere near a person who had been positively diagnosed. So when Diana was invited to attend the opening of the first AIDS ward in England at Middlesex Hospital, great speculation arose as to how she would handle the situation. When she shook hands with 12 AIDS patients without wearing gloves, the fear appeared to melt away for many others. "You could almost feel the taboos being broken," said Richard Kay, who covered the event for the *Daily Mail*. "I think of myself as a reasonably liberal, open-minded person, but nonetheless I was pretty amazed."[6]

So were professionals such as professor Michael Adler, who was working with AIDS patients at the time. Adler, who later served as the chief adviser on sexual health concerns for the British government, was taken aback by Diana's gesture, especially considering the impression many had about the disease being of a sexual nature limited to gay men. Adler believed that Diana brought a touch of humanity to the issue, dispelling myths in the process. During her trip to New York two years later, Diana spontaneously hugged a seven-year-old boy who had been diagnosed as HIV positive. "(Previously) people did not like the whole ambiance," Adler said. "It was seen to be mainly occurring amongst gay men and it involved sex, all the things we are not good at handling, but she actually cut through that. She gave it respectability and a profile."[7]

Some have suggested, or even claimed, that Diana's tender moments with the sick, or the dying, or the painfully poor were quite far from genuine. That she had always yearned to be loved—not only by a member of the opposite sex, but by the public—was unquestioned. The psychological trauma inflicted on her as a child, first when she rightly felt her parents' disappointment that she was born a girl, then when they separated and divorced, left her craving to be loved. She not only sought true romantic love from Charles and other men in her life, but she desired respect and admiration from people around the world. Critics who point to the orchestration surrounding Diana's charitable appearances claim that she was on her own personal stage, that she was the same girl who waved her arms on the diving board as a child and shouted, "Look at me, look at me!" They believe that the theatrics increased with time, that her performances became mechanical, almost robotic as she smiled for the cameras, and that her compassion for others increasingly became a show for the media and a cure for what ailed her emotionally.

Yet one couldn't express such an opinion to the parent of a sick child or an official from an AIDS ward of a hospital or a nameless, faceless starving African boy visited by Diana without receiving an angry response. They all believed that she truly cared. Many of them had witnessed phony performances before, and what better way to bring attention to a cause than to put on a show in front of a camera sending a picture to the entire world.

"Look, it doesn't really matter to me why she wanted to do this kind of thing," said Margaret Jay of Britain's National Aids Trust, not without a hint of anger. "We live in a world in which celebrities have a huge power to help organizations like mine. This one chose to and I'm grateful. End of story."[8]

STILL SEARCHING FOR LOVE

Diana could hardly be blamed for her desire to fill an emotional void. By 1989, her relationship with Hewitt was becoming a distant memory. And butler Paul Burrell was noting that on many nights the odometer on Prince Charles's vintage Aston Martin would have 22 miles added to it—the exact mileage of a round trip to Middlewich House, home of Camilla Parker Bowles. Burrell often received correspondences that Charles would be spending the night at a separate residence on particular evenings. On the rare occasions when Diana and Charles were together, terrible fights ensued. Burrell reported raised voices, slammed doors, then silence. Sometimes the battles grew violent. On one weekend night, he entered the sitting room, where he had set a table for two, only to see broken glass, spilled water, and Prince Charles on his hands and knees picking up silverware. Diana was nowhere in sight.

The lack of love from her husband continued to haunt Diana, who still hoped to win him over despite their sexual encounters with others. The psychological damage caused by her unfulfilling relationship with Charles caused Diana to seek happiness and tranquility through various questionable sources such as astrologers, masseurs, and even tarot card readers. She tried aromatherapy, hypnotherapy, and acupuncture in an attempt to find inner peace. Diana still held out hope for her marriage in the summer of 1989 despite all indications of its failings. Both her family and the royal family pressured her to work toward reconstructing her relationship with Charles. She even agreed to have another baby, but the marriage had been destroyed beyond repair. Any attempt to reconcile their differences resulted in more arguments, threats, and accusations.

In the fall of 1989, around the time Hewitt left for Germany, Diana became involved with old friend James Gilbey, whom she had met at age 17 and who had achieved wealth in dealing expensive used cars. Their relationship at first consisted mostly of complaining about love lives that had gone astray, but it soon grew into a romance. Gilbey spoke affectionately to Diana, even giving her the nickname "Squidgy." Their growing feelings were strongly suggested by a taped phone conversation on New Year's Eve that year in which both spoke of their feelings for each other, though it became apparent that he was far more taken with her than she was with him. The tape eventually landed in the eager hands of members of the media, who dubbed it "Squidgygate." It wasn't the only such tape in circulation. That same year a passionate and sexually explicit phone conversation between Camilla and Charles was recorded during which Charles claimed he wished to be a tampon. "Camillagate" was born.

Diana's relationship with Gilbey flourished in late 1989, but she still pined for Hewitt. Even the New Year's Eve conversation revealed that Gilbey felt far more passionately about her than she did about him. She spoke about her appreciation for Gilbey, but he called her "darling" throughout the conversation, an expression of love she didn't return. In fact, if Squidgygate revealed anything, it was that Diana considered Gilbey as little more than a trusted friend, though she was heard to blow kisses to him over the phone. Additionally, the possibility that she engaged in a sexual relationship with Gilbey to replace the one she had lost with Hewitt can't be discounted. The conversation eventually drifted toward her relationship with the royal family, which was certainly not helped by another tense holiday season. Diana complained that she had been overcome by sadness, that she felt restricted by the confines of her marriage, and that Charles made her life a "real torture."[9]

An event that occurred a week after William's eighth birthday in late June 1990 served to signal the end of any attempt to reconcile. Charles broke his right arm when he tumbled off his polo pony. He was eventually informed that the arm wasn't healing properly, whereupon he was taken to the Queen's Medical Centre in Nottingham for surgery. Diana welcomed the opportunity to pick him up from the hospital and take him home, where she could show her concern while nursing him back to health. But as she attempted to mother him, he utterly rejected her and told her he wanted to be left alone. As she drove back to London in tears, Camilla arrived at Highgrove to be by his side. Burrell recalled Charles's joy at seeing her. Burrell expressed his view that the royal marriage was officially doomed from that moment.

By August the world had turned its attention to the Middle East. The Iraqi invasion and brutal takeover of Kuwait prompted Great Britain and dozens of other nations to contribute to an American-led troop surge in Saudi Arabia, as well as on the Persian Gulf and Red Sea. Before Christmas, Diana had renewed her affair with Hewitt, who had returned home from Germany. But he was sent to the Persian Gulf in January, when Operation Desert Storm began. Diana sometimes mailed him as many as four passionate letters a day, expressing her longing for him and a deep disappointment that she remained in a dishonest marriage. She also wrote about the anger she felt that the relationship between Charles and Camilla had yet to be noted by the media, a fact that resulted in increased frustration for her over time.

Diana's feelings for Hewitt became public during the Gulf War through his estranged girlfriend Emma Stewardson, who revealed to *News of the World* that the princess had been sending gifts and love letters to the major. Though Stewardson didn't claim a sexual relationship between the two, the media reports frightened Diana. After all, it was her husband's infidelities, certainly not her own, that she wanted publicized. When Hewitt returned from the war, he visited Diana at Highgrove. Press scrutiny had become so intense that he felt compelled to hide in the trunk of the car en route to see her. Things would get far less comfortable. The pressure to prevent further suspicion motivated Diana to distance herself from Hewitt, who in turn felt rejected. Rather than phoning him or meeting him in private to let him down gently, she simply stopped taking his calls.

The Gulf War had been won, but the war between Diana and Charles was still being waged. On June 3, 1991, both were informed that son William had been struck in the head with a golf club at his boarding school. They raced to Royal Berkshire Hospital and were comforted by seeing William sitting up and alert in his bed. He had suffered what was described to them by his doctor as a depressed fracture in the forehead. William was relocated to Great Ormond Street Hospital for surgery. Diana and Charles were told the operation was not risky, whereupon Charles decided to keep his evening and morning appointments before returning to see William following the surgery. All hell broke loose in the media. Both the *Daily Mirror* and the *Sun* chastised Charles for leaving while his wife remained by William's side. Diana later complained that her husband had accused her of exaggerating the severity of their son's injury to reporters, which in turn made him appear uncaring. Gilbey later reported that Diana was horrified both by the accident and by the prince's supposed lack of concern about it. She even told friend Adrian Ward-Jackson, "I can't be with someone who behaves like that."[10]

The media often praised Diana's feelings for her two sons while down-playing those of Charles, despite the fact that there has been ample evidence to suggest that both were loving parents. On one occasion when the couple returned from an official visit to Canada, photographers snapped pictures of William throwing himself into the embrace of his mother. Seconds later, more were taken of Charles throwing his arms out to greet the boys. Yet the only photos used by the British media were those of Diana giddily waiting to hug her children. In fact, the photo of Diana was among the most famous of her married life.

A MARRIAGE DOOMED TO FAIL

Aside from being together in their official capacities, Diana was rarely with Charles after all emotional ties had been broken. That truth had been brought home to butler Paul Burrell when he accompanied the couple to Japan in November 1990. He saw them as nothing more than business associates spending time together only because of their work duties. They even stayed in separate rooms. Burrell felt no closeness between them and was particularly taken aback by Diana's quick temper and touchiness over the slightest details. It was the first time he had felt uncomfortable in her presence. It became obvious that not only did she no longer have feelings for Charles, but she had also become fed up with the strict scheduling and protocol required of her as the Princess of Wales.

Meanwhile, Burrell noted the humiliating effect on Diana when Charles consistently criticized her appearance and performance. Perhaps because Diana was well known for being fashion-conscious, Charles took every opportunity to insult her taste in clothing. On an official trip to Czechoslovakia in May 1991, in which they stayed not only in separate quarters but on separate floors of President Havel's ornate Prague palace, Diana was attired in an all black-and-white outfit for an afternoon event. Charles quipped, "You look like you've just joined the Mafia" in front of Diana and all the attending officials.[11] If his intention was to draw laughter, he failed completely. If his intention was to humiliate his wife, he succeeded.

By this time, it was impossible to look at the royal marriage with rose-colored glasses, though most casual observers and even those who closely scrutinized the relationship believed that divorce remained unthinkable. But new financial adviser Joseph Sanders, as well as old friend and adviser Dr. James Colthurst, began preparing Diana for a separation from Charles that would still cast her in a positive light. An outlet for such a scenario would reveal itself in the form of a biography about Diana written by freelance journalist Andrew Morton, who had previously covered the royal family in the newspapers. Colthurst knew Morton quite well—in fact, they often competed against each other in games of squash. He made arrangements to meet with Morton over breakfast, during which they discussed the misery experienced by Diana revolving around her failing marriage, her bulimia, and other mental and emotional problems. They spoke about her negative feelings regarding her treatment by the royal family, and they discussed the affair between Charles and Camilla Parker Bowles, which Diana considered the ruination of their relationship. In a nation always fascinated by news of the royal family and in a world that adored the princess, revelations such as Charles's affair and Diana's failed suicide attempts had to make the book a runaway bestseller.

All Morton needed were the thoughts of Diana. Colthurst informed the princess about the plans for a biography, but she hesitated. Rather than simply think things through, she decided to find the answer in the stars. Colthurst tracked down friend Felix Lyle to perform an astrological reading for Diana. Though Diana knew astrologers of her own, Lyle would provide an objective astrological view, if there is such a thing. They spoke about the deviousness of Neptune and the strength of Pluto in her chart before Lyle and the princess announced that the planets and stars aligned favorably. The biography was a go.

Morton never interviewed Diana, who demanded that she remain blameless for any backlash. She could deny any involvement in the book, which would place complete responsibility on Morton. She wanted the opportunity to tell Charles and members of the royal family that the book had been written without her consent. Diana and Colthurst then created tape recordings that were given to Morton, who followed up with further questions for the princess. She gave him permission to interview her friends. Though Hewitt turned down the opportunity to speak with Morton, friends such as Gilbey and Bartholomew quickly accepted.

The world was about to discover what Diana and Charles strongly suspected from the time of their honeymoon more than a decade earlier—that their marriage was a failure. Much to the delight of those who idolized the princess or who lapped up every juicy tidbit of information about the royal family, they were going to find out why.

NOTES

1. Andrew Morton, *Diana: Her True Story* (New York: Simon and Schuster, 1997), 104.

2. Ibid., 63.

3. "Touched by Royalty: Remembering Princess Diana's visit to Henry Street 18 years ago," March 29, 2007, http://www.henrystreet.org/site/News2?JservSessionIdr007=jtv4qstpt2.app26a&page=NewsArticle&id=9278&news_iv_ctrl=0 (accessed October 26, 2007).

4. Tina Brown, *The Diana Chronicles* (New York: Doubleday, 2007), 283.

5. P. D. Jephson, *Shadows of a Princess* (New York: HarperCollins, 2006), 46.

6. Rosalind Coward, *Diana: The Portrait* (Riverside, N.J.: Andrews McMeel Publishing, 2004), 179.

7. Ibid.

8. Tim Clayton and Phil Craig, *Diana: Story of a Princess* (New York: Simon and Schuster, 2001), 185.

9. Sally Bedell Smith, *Diana in Search of Herself* (New York: Times Books, 1999), 201.

10. Ibid., 208.

11. Paul Burrell, *A Royal Duty* (New York: G. P. Putnam's Sons, 2003), 134.

Chapter 10

THEIR SEPARATE WAYS

While Morton was busy writing a biography that would expose, among other details, the love affair between Charles and Camilla, photographs published by the *Daily Mail* showed that Diana's relationship wasn't the only royal marriage in trouble. Pictures had been found of Sarah, Duchess of York, with Texas multimillionaire Steve Wyatt, son of Saks Fifth Avenue heiress Lynn Sakowitz Wyatt. Sarah and Andrew announced their separation in mid-March 1990.

By the time those photographs were published, however, Sarah had already become involved with another wealthy Texan, John Bryan. An Italian photographer followed the couple to a secluded holiday spot and snapped more than 200 pictures of them kissing, including one in which Bryan was kissing the tops of her feet. The *Mirror* purchased more than 50 of the photos, one of which became known as the "toe-sucking picture."[1]

Though Diana and Sarah had had their differences since the latter joined the royal family, both appeared to be heading in the same direction. In fact, it was speculated that Sarah was encouraging Diana to separate from her husband just as she had severed her relationship with Andrew. Diana's marriage to Charles certainly appeared to be on its last legs during a February 1992 tour of India in which he didn't accompany her to the famed Taj Mahal. Photographers flocked to snap pictures of Diana and all but ignored Charles, who was speaking at a business forum. Though images of Diana standing all alone in front of a symbol of love such as the Taj Mahal, which was built by a Mogul emperor for his wife, could prove depressing and a testimony to a failing marriage, she didn't seem to mind.

In fact, she appeared to welcome the impression that the fairy tale marriage had come crashing down.

Photographer Jayne Fincher asked Diana her thoughts about the Taj Mahal, to which she gave a bit of a coded answer, speaking about the healing qualities of the monument. Media members quickly picked up on the message that she required such a thoughtful moment at the Taj Mahal to rid her mind of the treatment she was receiving from her husband. After a polo match Charles competed in two days later, Diana, who was supposed to present prizes to the winning team, uttered a far more direct rebuff of her husband. Diana sidled up to a staff member and voiced her concern that she wasn't certain she could kiss Charles in public. When Charles scored a goal, he walked over to Diana. It was the eve of Valentine's Day and everyone expected one whopper of a smooch. Instead, Diana turned her head and was pecked on the neck. The next day, newspapers around the world reported that the bad kiss symbolized an even worse marriage.

The following month Diana's father, Johnnie Spencer, died suddenly of a heart attack at Humana Hospital Wellington in north London. The tragedy was quite shocking considering he had only been suffering from mild pneumonia. Diana had visited him just four days earlier with William. She planned on flying home from a family skiing trip without Charles, but he and his staff members tried to convince her to fly with him for the sake of public perception. It took the queen's persuasion for Diana to give in. Yet despite his urgings that he and Diana should accompany each other, Charles bolted to Highgrove upon arrival, leaving her to grieve for her departed father alone. The prince flew in by helicopter for the funeral on April 1, then departed for London rather than attend the cremation. It was during the funeral, however, that one grand, silent gesture ended her feud with Raine, who was understandably devastated by her husband's unexpected passing. Diana was quite far away from Raine during the ceremony, but the princess left her seat, sidled up to her stepmother, took her hand, and walked through the church with her. Frances Shand Kydd, on the other hand, made herself quite unnoticeable at the funeral.

Meanwhile, Diana began getting cold feet as the publication of her biography neared. Initially, she had anticipated its arrival with relish, as her desire to expose the love affair of Charles and Camilla was finally to be realized. But a month before it was to be released she became apprehensive and worried over the possibility of a negative reaction not only from the media and the public but also from family and friends. She even admitted her fear to film producer David Puttnam during a March dinner party at which she spoke about the horrors of AIDS. She began by spewing out to him the failures of her marriage, then confided in him that a book had been written that she hoped would clear the air but might instead cause major problems. "Now I think it was a very stupid thing that will cause all kinds of terrible trouble," Diana said, according to Puttnam. "I would like to reel the movie back. It is the daftest thing I have ever done."[2]

THE TELL-ALL TALE

The world would soon be the judge of just how daft it was. The *Sunday Times* announced that it would serialize the book starting on June 7. Newspaper editor Andrew Neil could hardly believe his eyes when he began reading excerpts of Morton's book. He was floored by the revelations. He remained skeptical about its accuracy until Morton went over the sources of the book with him and assured him that there were many more. It took guts for the *Sunday Times* to publish such a powerful condemnation of Prince Charles and the royal family, but the paper still paid the British equivalent of $440,000 for the rights to print it. The newspaper plastered posters on roadsides and ran television advertisements trumpeting the serialization of the book. Rival publications set out to plant doubt about the authenticity of the book by claiming it had no royal authorization, but their efforts failed.

The first excerpt detailed Diana's bulimia, her half-hearted suicide attempts, and, of course, the relationship between Charles and Camilla. Overwhelming fear prompted Diana to alternately spin in both directions. According to *Daily Mirror* editor Richard Stott, she told photographer Kent Gavin that she had in no way cooperated with the writing of the book, a claim that newspaper ran with in a screaming page-one headline on June 8. Morton soon lived up to his end of the deal with Diana by taking full responsibility for the contents of the book, which in turn served to undermine his efforts. After all, how credible would a biography of Diana be without the input of Diana herself?

Press Complaints Commission Chairman Lord McGregor sought to find out. He contacted Robert Fellowes, Diana's brother-in-law, who had served as the queen's private secretary for 15 years. Diana repeated, this time to Fellowes, her assertion that she had nothing to do with the book. Fellowes and the queen's press secretary, Charles Anson, relayed that denial to McGregor, who, without condemning Morton specifically, then issued a statement claiming that all press coverage of the royal marriage had been an "odious exhibition of journalists dabbling their fingers in the stuff of other people's souls."[3]

As excerpts of the book continued to run, however, it became apparent that Diana had indeed contributed greatly to its content. The media were tipped off about a trip she was about to make to visit Bartholomew, who had been quoted in the book on the subject of the princess's bulimia. When photos of the two chatting appeared in British tabloids, there could no longer be any doubt. McGregor, Fellowes, and others who felt deceived by Diana were angry with her for denying her role in Morton's biography. This knowledge of Diana's role in the book led her to feel overwhelmed at the prospect of accompanying the royal family on all the annual summer events.

Members of the British press lambasted Morton and his collaborators, portraying their work as mostly fiction. They criticized the *Sunday Times* for running the excerpts. Their angry reaction was greatly motivated by a code of many British journalists that the royal family is sacred. One writer claimed Morton was more interested in money than in the survival of the royal family. Others still refused to believe that Diana contributed to the contents of the book.

The princess was worried about public reaction, but that fear was allayed on a June 12 visit to a Merseyside hospice, her first official engagement since the excerpts hit the newsstands. As she appeared before a waiting public, a crowd numbering in the thousands cheered her. An elderly woman sweetly stroked her face, which prompted Diana to cry uncontrollably. The tears came not only from the gesture and a feeling of oneness with the people, but from all the pain she had experienced over the years. It was a release of emotions that had been bottled up inside her.

Charles had some emotions to deal with as well after reading the excerpts in the newspaper. He had hoped against hope that only Diana's friends and not his wife had contributed such accusatory passages. Charles had already spoken to the queen about a possible separation from Diana after the kiss-on-the-neck incident in India, but he was asked to grin and bear it for another six months. The revelations in Morton's book, however, killed that idea. Though based on past traditions and the urgings of such revered friends as Lord Mountbatten, the infidelity of a prince is far from shameful; the notion of criticizing and revealing secrets about the royal family was considered unforgivable.

A hastily called meeting with the queen and the Duke of Edinburgh was arranged at Windsor Castle on June 15, the day before the book was to be published. Though Diana's involvement in the book could hardly be denied, she reiterated that contention. But there was no turning back at that point. She refused to apologize for anything she had done. She expressed her hatred for Camilla, and she told her powerful in-laws that she wanted a trial separation. The reply was sharp and immediate. The queen and Prince Philip demanded that through compromise and unselfish approaches to their marriage, they must work out their differences for the sake of their children, the royal family, and the country. Diana later admitted that the confrontation proved to be a relief. For years she couldn't summon the courage to express her feelings about Charles, Camilla, and her relationship with the royal family to the royal family. Now that everything was out in the open, Diana felt more at ease.

The queen hoped to discuss the situation further. She scheduled another meeting for the following day, but Diana chose not to attend. She did, however, correspond often with Prince Philip, who took the lead as mediator. In fact, the duke appeared more resolute about saving the marriage than did his son. But Diana was angered by the tone of the messages sent to her by her father-in-law, who asked in no uncertain terms for her to rethink how she had performed in her marriage. One note from Philip claimed that while Diana was to be commended for her charity work and solo tours, being the wife of Prince Charles "involved much more than simply being a hero with the British people."[4] Diana was insulted by the correspondences, particularly since she had gained great respect for Prince Philip over the years. The Duke of Edinburgh was merely warming up. He added that jealousy had diseased the marriage, which Diana interpreted as a slam against her. But then, how does a woman prevent herself from being jealous when her husband continues a love affair with another? Diana was taken aback when he had what she considered to be the temerity to write that her husband had made "a considerable sacrifice" when he cut off his relationship with Camilla initially and followed that up by asking her, "Can you honestly look into your heart and say that Charles' relationship with Camilla had nothing to do with your behavior towards him in your marriage?"[5]

By that summer, however, the open communication shifted their views of each other. Diana's retorts to Prince Philip's comments increased his respect for her. His notes began taking on a friendlier tone. She felt vindicated when a member of the royal family actually admitted that her anger was based on legitimate concerns and was not the product of a raving maniac. She appreciated the attempt to understand her and even flirted with the idea that someday her marriage to Charles could be revived. But at that time, she believed the separation to be necessary.

Any thought of a healthy marital relationship was naïve, especially after Morton's bombshell bestseller hit the shelves and the ensuing media circus began. The *Sunday Times* attempted in vain to pry a response to the book out of Charles, but it did run a story on June 28 quoting his friends as saying the prince was annoyed that Diana still denied full cooperation with Morton. They further stated that Charles simply wanted Diana to admit her involvement and that it was a mistake. Later that summer, tabloids ran the Squidgygate tapes, and an article in the *Sun* stated plainly that Diana had maintained a physical relationship with James Hewitt. She launched a lawsuit against the paper, which she never took to court. Now that the media had reported the possible infidelity of Diana with both Gilbey and Hewitt, her indignity over Charles's relationship with Camilla was called into question. Friends reported that she was badly hurt by the negative press.

LAST LEGS OF A ROYAL MARRIAGE

The Prince and Princess of Wales attended their official engagements that autumn with an undisguised chilliness toward each other. Both had met with lawyers about a possible separation or divorce, and friends on both sides admitted that their personal contacts with each other most often resulted in raised voices and hurt feelings. Diana initially backed out of an official trip accompanying Charles to Korea, but the queen convinced her to reconsider. The princess attended, but made no attempt to hide her lack of enthusiasm during the visit. Charles's morose demeanor added to an overall picture that prompted tabloids to nickname them "The Glums."[6] Charles wrote to a friend and spoke of his anguish and his utterly miserable outlook of the future.

Soon thereafter, another in the seemingly endless published reports regarding the indiscretions of the royal family hit the newsstands when the *Daily Mirror* and the *Sun* ran excerpts of the sexually charged conversation between Charles and Camilla that quickly became known as "Camillagate." The lurid dialogue not only confirmed the prince's infidelity, but also called into question his suitability to be king of England.

And as if public opinion of the monarchy hadn't dipped low enough, a blaze that swept through Windsor Castle on November 24 added fire to the fire. The ruination of the royal marriage through infidelity and backstabbing had most British citizens disgusted, but when it was suggested that they pay for the destruction through additional taxes, resentment boiled over. Already a controversial issue was whether the queen should pay taxes at all. The flames caused an estimated $40 million–$80 million in damages. The citizens wondered why their financial burdens should be increased when the woman who symbolized the royal family was not required to put forth a shilling.

Meanwhile, neither Charles nor Diana was in the mood for compromise when they squabbled over which parent would accompany William and Harry on the weekend of November 19. The royal family had assumed the boys would attend their father's shooting party, but Diana had planned to spend time with them alone, for she admitted that she could not bear to spend a weekend with her husband. And during such a sensitive period, she certainly didn't want to be surrounded by his friends. The flap turned out to be the final straw. Charles had hemmed and hawed over the possibility of a legal separation, greatly due to the insistence of his family that matters with Diana be smoothed over, but his anger won out. Charles told Diana of his decision at Kensington Palace on November 25. The princess agreed immediately to separate and appeared that evening to be quite content, even downright happy, according to newspaper accounts. But James Hewitt detected quite a different tone from Diana during a phone conversation that night. "Diana sounded flat and low," Hewitt said. "She did not think that it would ever be possible for her to have what she really wanted."[7]

What did Diana want? She had often spoken to friends about how she envied them. All she had ever yearned for, she told them, was to be truly loved, even in a life far simpler than that to which she had become accustomed as princess. The modest existence now was out of the question, even after a divorce that took four years to play out. Diana would remain one of the most recognized and revered women on the planet. As for unquestioned, undying love, she would seek that for the rest of a life that proved tragically short.

While Diana continued seeking happiness and fulfillment, British prime minister John Major read a prepared statement to members of parliament. "It is announced from Buckingham Palace that, with regret, the Prince and Princess of Wales decided to separate," Major said. "Their Royal Highnesses have no plans to divorce and their constitutional positions are unaffected. This decision has been reached amicably and they will both continue to participate fully in the upbringing of their children. . . . Their Royal Highnesses will continue to carry out full and separate programmes of public engagements and will, from time to time, attend family occasions and national events together."[8]

Major then drew a collective gasp when he added that divorce was out of the question and that Charles and Diana remained in line to serve as, respectively, king and queen of England. Most believed the notion ridiculous that a couple living apart and taking every opportunity as individuals to verbally bash their spouse should even be considered heirs to the throne, particularly at that moment. The archbishop of Canterbury, the man who would eventually crown the couple, suggested two stipulations: that both maintain close bonds to their sons and that all love affairs be kept under wraps. The first would be no problem. The second wouldn't even be attempted.

Following the separation announcement, lawyers on both sides worked feverishly to strike the best deal for their clients. Diana certainly didn't mind when it was insisted that all solo trips in her role as Princess of Wales not be made as an official representative of the queen. The dual custody arrangement left Diana in daily care of William and Harry. After a battle over living arrangements, she gained residency of a spacious Kensington Palace apartment. She would no longer be forced to take a weekly excursion to Highgrove, which filled her with such terrible memories. And though the financial aspects of the relationship would not be ironed out until their divorce in 1996, Diana was certainly well compensated.

Friends described Diana immediately following the separation as far more content and relaxed. She laughed easily and often during a ski vacation in Colorado with personal trainer Jenny Rivett, who was surprised that the princess took her up on the offer. Rivett reported that Diana dreaded the thought of spending the time between Christmas and New Year's as a separated wife, but that she concluded the trip by exclaiming that she had experienced one of her most joyful holidays ever.

Diana was wealthy, famous, loved, and on her own. And she remained in charge of the children she so adored. At 31 years old, she was eager to learn what life had to offer, both professionally and personally. A cover story by Anthony Holden in the February 1993 issue of *Vanity Fair*, titled "Di's Palace Coup," described the difference in the Diana tied down to Charles and the one who was suddenly free. Holden wrote of a long-unseen bounce in her step and a gleam in her eye. Meanwhile, another publication had placed another stake in her husband's reputation. A month earlier, the Camillagate tapes, of which the British public had only been given a glimpse in November, were published in their entirety. Diana's image as a victim of Charles's adultery had been solidified. She had always been the favorite between the two, around the world as well as in Britain, particularly among women. Now, even though the public had been made to suspect her own infidelities with Hewitt, the sensationally explicit sexual phone banter between Charles and Camilla in 1989 confirmed that he had jumped first into an affair.

Even if Charles and Diana had begun their unfaithful relationships simultaneously, the damage to the former was destined to be greater. Charles, after all, had been raised in the royal family. Though he had no intention of allowing such transgressions to become public, the mere fact that he had participated in such a lowbrow, sexually oriented conversation destroyed his fervent desire to be taken seriously. Charles yearned for respect for his views on both political and philosophical matters. His stated fantasy of being turned into a tampon so he could always be "close" to Camilla was certainly not about to bring him that respect. Granted, it is quite likely that other well-respected leaders in world history have partaken in rather adolescent sexual talk, but they weren't caught. And perception in his case was everything. Charles was simply devastated by such revelations.

The perception of Diana, on the other hand, was barely damaged. Not only were her infidelities not yet confirmed, but her image had been cemented as a victim of Charles's alleged cavalier attitude toward unfaithfulness and the resulting pain he inflicted upon her. Women rushed to her defense, declaring the princess a symbol of female victimization. Diana soaked it all in gladly. The joy she experienced on the skiing trip shortly after the separation was announced continued. She finally felt unshackled, as she was no longer tied down by the constraints in her daily routine that had previously been placed on her by the traditions of the royal family. And she thoroughly enjoyed styling Kensington Apartments Eight and Nine to her own taste.

Diana's staff included butler Paul Burrell, whom she requested to move with her to Kensington. The shock of the separation affected Burrell, who at first strongly disliked the idea but eventually grew to be one of Diana's strongest supporters. He was permitted to act with far less formality at Kensington than he was at Highgrove. Visitors noted a more relaxed and friendly environment, both in how the home was decorated and in the manner in which they were treated. Guests arrived to the enticing sound of classical music and the aroma of sweet-smelling flowers. Diana replaced Charles's drab military paintings and architecture with lighter touches such as soothing landscapes. "There was a lot more banter and laughter, not so much creeping around," explained one friend. "Even the cleaners say hello."9

Though she did her best to give Kensington her own touch, with a focused eye on making her sons feel comfortable, something inside Diana pushed for a clean break. She began yearning for her own home in the country, free from all ties to her royal past. Though she was separated from Charles, she still remained under the constant watchful eyes of guards outside Kensington Palace with a staff taking care of her every need. She recalled her times at Coleherne Court as unburdened and fun. She understood that her personal and professional responsibilities had grown tremendously, but she still felt a strong attraction to the idea of cutting her royal ties, at least in reference to her residence, and moving into a simpler and less conspicuous home. Her lone concern was the certainty of strong condemnation from the royal family, the media, and the British public at such an undisguised split from the royal life she had led for more than a decade. But no matter how she attempted to transform Kensington Palace into a home of her own, a rather sickening feeling washed over her every time she returned from one of her increasingly frequent weekend getaways to the homes of friends. Every reminder of the prince had been tossed out or sent to him at his new home at St. James, but the couple had spent so much time at Kensington Palace over the years that the bitter memories simply couldn't be removed. "I wake up on Sunday morning and I dread going back," Diana told friends. "It's like returning to prison."[10]

NEW BEAU, BUT NO NEW HOME

It appeared in April 1993 that brother Charles was about to hand her a "get out of jail free" card. He offered her a house on the Althorp estate, a comparatively modest four-bedroom property known as the Garden House. Diana had fretted the notion of being considered extravagant, especially now that she was only a fringe member of the royal family. That fear had even motivated her to unload her expensive Mercedes after the separation had become official. She felt a rush of excitement over the idea of decorating her very own home for the first time in her life. After all, Kensington could hardly be considered her own, and her apartment at Coleherne Court had been shared with roommates. But alas, the plans fell through when her brother decided that police surveillance and media interest would preclude any possibility of peace and quiet. Diana was angry at Charles for yanking away his offer without discussing his change of mind with her. She penned two letters begging him to reconsider, but received no reply. Diana had spent a great deal of time planning her new home, all in vain. Her relationship with her brother remained strained for quite some time following that incident.

Meanwhile, her relationship with handsome, debonair art dealer Oliver Hoare was heating up, despite his marriage to French heiress Diane de Waldner, with whom Diana claimed he was no longer in love. Critics claimed the princess seriously began dating Hoare because he was a close friend of Charles's and she still sought revenge for her estranged husband's affair with Camilla. Hoare had a great deal in common with the prince, including a passion for art and literature. He had something else in common with Charles—a penchant for infidelity. He wed Waldner in 1976, but had a long affair with a Turkish woman named Ayesha Gul, who was also married. Hoare and his wife had befriended Charles and Diana, as well as Andrew and Camilla Parker Bowles, in the mid-1980s.

Diana had developed more than a friendship with Hoare just before her separation became official. Though she attempted to keep the relationship secret, Diana's protection officer Ken Wharfe offered that those at heavily guarded Kensington Palace had become aware of it when she tried to sneak Hoare in through the courtyard of Princess Margaret's apartment with a blanket over his head. In the afternoons they would meet quite openly for lunch at San Lorenzo, which was owned by a woman who opened up her nearby apartment to them after meals. Diana and her new beau played games of cat and mouse with photographers attempting to snap photos of the two. Confronted about her relationship with a married man, Diana claimed Hoare had promised to leave his wife and run away with her to Italy to begin a new life. Wharfe concurred that Diana was quite taken with the wealthy art dealer. Close friend and healer Simone Simmons tried to convince Diana that Hoare was merely making promises he had no intention of keeping. "He's going to marry me," the princess insisted. "Yes, and pigs might fly," Simmons replied.[11]

Diana wondered if she would ever find true and lasting love. Hoare would fail to provide it, adding to what was growing into a depressingly long list.

NOTES

1. Sally Bedell Smith, *Diana in Search of Herself* (New York: Times Books, 1999), 242.

2. Ibid., 222.

3. Andrew Morton, *Diana: Her True Story* (New York: Simon and Schuster, 1997), 215.

4. Paul Burrell, *A Royal Duty* (New York: G. P. Putnam's Sons, 2003), 161.

5. Ibid., 162.

6. Smith, *Diana in Search of Herself*, 232.

7. Anne Pasternak, *Princess in Love* (paperback) (New York: Penguin USA, 1994), 297.

8. House of Commons Hansard Debates for December 9, 1992, Publications and Records, *Prince and Princess of Wales*, December 9, 1992, http://www.pub lications.parliament.uk/pa/cm199293/cmhansrd/1992–12–09/debate-1.html (accessed November 1, 2007).

9. Andrew Morton, *Diana: Her New Life* (New York: Simon and Schuster, 1994), 60.

10. Ibid., 65.

11. Simone Simmons, *Diana: The Last Word* (New York: St. Martin's Press, 2005), 58.

Chapter 11

STILL CHASING A DREAM

Diana was persistent—too persistent—in her desire to hold on to Hoare. She had spoken with Hoare's wife, Diane, on many occasions, pawning off her relationship with him as merely a friendship. But Diane became leery when the tone of their phone conversations changed. Diana became quite abrupt, and the frequency of her calls increased, leading Diane to suspect that Oliver and the princess had indeed engaged in an affair. After all, had he not already enjoyed a long-term sexual relationship with Gul? Diane didn't directly challenge her husband. She did, however, demand that he limit his time with Diana and let her know in no uncertain terms that the phone calls must cease. Diana continued the correspondence, sometimes calling three or four times a day and simply hanging up if Diane answered.

The princess pleaded with Hoare to continue their relationship not because of the physical contact, but rather for her emotional needs. They discussed his wife's concerns, but Diana cried out, "Doesn't she understand what I'm going through? Doesn't she know that I need your help and advice with all the terrible problems I'm having? . . . Doesn't Diane realize that I have no one to whom I can turn? No one whom I can trust? You are my only friend. Doesn't she realize that I am so bitterly alone?"[1] The pulling in two directions took a toll on Hoare, who began to withdraw. But the less Hoare saw of Diana, the more desperate she became and the more she called him. She often didn't speak, as her sole purpose was to hear his soothing voice.

Diana's behavior around Oliver Hoare was understandably criticized. After all, had she not suffered tremendous emotional trauma over Charles's affair with Camilla? Now she was the Camilla of this relationship. Though speculation that the excitement surrounding the new freedom afforded her by the separation prompted her questionable conduct, Diana did beg Hoare to keep his promise to leave his wife. Early on she joked about their nearly identical first names and how if Hoare called out her name in bed, his wife Diane wouldn't suspect a thing. But soon Diana became quite possessive of her beau and began insisting on exclusive rights to Hoare, which sent him scurrying. He began missing scheduled engagements with her before he stopped seeing her completely. The confused Hoare also left his wife for two months before moving back.

Diane received one particularly nasty call in the fall of 1993, which she suspected was made by Diana. Diane had been shocked and angered by similar calls, though this one was particularly severe, so she insisted her husband call British Telecom for a tracing of the calls. Oliver Hoare acceded to her request, believing that Diana could never have spoken with such venom to his wife. The phone company installed a tracking device on the Hoares' phone. The calls stopped for a couple months, but then six calls were made on January 13, 1994. Other calls also came in that week. British Telecom showed Oliver Hoare one number, which he recognized immediately as Diana's personal number at Kensington Palace. The police informed Buckingham Palace, after which the queen's personal secretary, Robert Fellowes, spoke with Diana. The calls abruptly ended, which caused Oliver and Diane Hoare to drop the matter.

The media, however, had a field day. The *News of the World* ran a story about Diana's phone calls to Hoare, whereupon she reacted angrily toward reporters and photographers who besieged her. Hoare told reporters that both he and Diane knew there was nothing improper about his relationship with Diana, but the incident made Diana look desperate and childish. She told the *Daily Mail* royal correspondent that she had been framed. "What are they trying to do to me?" she asked. "I feel I am being destroyed. There is no truth to it."[2] She further insisted that although she did call Hoare, the nature of the calls was not as alleged. Diana also opened up her engagement book and pointed to several dates in which she was accused of having called Hoare, but she asserted that her whereabouts would have made it impossible. She later told friend Joseph Sanders that she had indeed made the calls, not only from her home but also at various phone booths while wearing disguises. Though many among the British public believed Diana did harass Diane Hoare, they blamed her fragile emotional state following the separation.

Soon Diana was to be vilified for another past relationship. The beau in question was Hewitt, who by 1994 was looking to cash in on his affair with Diana. Hewitt had become fearful when told of tape recordings and photos in newspaper safes that would link him to the princess. The rumors about their relationship had played a role in his crumbling military career despite the fact that he had distinguished himself as a brave and effective soldier during the Gulf War. He needed the money, and both the tabloids and publishers were offering plenty. Hewitt soon met with *Daily Express* journalist Diana Pasternak to find out what the media knew, but the strategy backfired. Not only did he discover little, but Pasternak learned a great deal about his affair with Diana. Hewitt soon found out that the writer was busily penning a book about the relationship titled *Princess in Love*, which would be published in time for the holiday buying rush. The press uniformly labeled Hewitt a money-grubbing cad, though his claims of a sexual relationship with Diana were splashed all over the tabloids. Most believed that as a representative of the British military, he should have had a sense of honor that would have prevented him from staining the reputation of a woman in line to be queen.

Diana was understandably nervous when Pasternak's book hit the shelves. But she did more than heave a sigh of relief when she feasted her eyes on a headline in the October 8, 1994, edition of the *Daily Mirror* that claimed Diana was blameless for her actions. She let out a joyful scream. A poll in that same newspaper revealed that only 27 percent of its readers blamed Diana for her affair with Hewitt, and a mere 15 percent responded that their opinion of the princess had been tarnished. A surprising 81 percent believed Charles had driven her into the arms of another man, and 61 percent offered that the couple should divorce immediately. The publicity had also severely damaged the reputation of the monarchy. A disturbing 73 percent of those polled felt that Queen Elizabeth II should be the last British monarch.

CHARLES'S SIDE OF THE STORY

Hewitt wasn't the only man in Diana's life to create controversy. In early 1994, British television personality Jonathan Dimbleby was preparing both a documentary and a biography about Prince Charles that both believed would vindicate him after all the accusations about his treatment of Diana spewed forth in Andrew Morton's book. Diana grew quite concerned over the contents of the work, though Dimbleby attempted to ease her mind during a meeting in March. The filmed conversation between Dimbleby and the prince cast his performance in that role in a positive light, but most memorable was Charles's answer to accusations of infidelity previous to the separation. The prince claimed that the accusations he was consistently unfaithful were false and that only when both he and the princess deemed the marriage an irretrievable failure did he stray, though he neglected to cite Camilla Parker Bowles by name. The documentary, which aired on the night of June 29, was seen by 63 percent of the British viewing audience. Among those who didn't watch was Diana, who instead attended a fund-raising dinner at a London gallery wearing a revealing, sexy black dress that stole some of the thunder of the documentary in media reports the following day. The princess did admit later, however, to having taped the Dimbleby interview with her estranged husband.

Both the television program and the book brought sympathy to Charles. And although they also revealed indiscretions in her personal life, Diana discovered with great relief that she was still loved in Britain and around the world. Such had been the case since the separation was announced. No longer forced to display an emotional attachment to Charles, she was free to be herself on solo tours to Zimbabwe and Nepal in early 1993. She served more as a British ambassador than as a representative of the royal family, a role she greatly preferred. She became more involved with the International Red Cross and also toiled to increase awareness of AIDS and poverty in underdeveloped nations. She continued her work with the homeless. The abolishment of land mines also became a pet project. Diana even worked with women who had suffered, as she had, with eating disorders.

Though highly successful, her trip to Zimbabwe proved quite frustrating. On a visit to a hospice for children stricken by AIDS, Diana was overcome with emotion. She cried when she learned that none of the kids were expected to reach the age of six. Photos taken later in the trip of Diana hovering over a huge pot and doling out food to hungry children proved quite touching, but she understood that she would soon return to her life of wealth and ease while these same youngsters were doomed to severe poverty. Again, those close to her duly noted her genuine reaction to the plight of those far less fortunate. "Those who believe that Diana's work was nothing more than a series of photo opportunities in glamorous locations around the world should have seen this drained, exhausted woman sitting in the back of the helicopter that day and heard her speak of the heart-breaking scenes she had just witnessed," said Ken Wharfe.[3]

She attempted to throw herself into her work, even taking lessons to increase her effectiveness as a public speaker. Diana hired former soap opera actor Peter Settelin, who taught her to talk more conversationally. She used the instruction during a speech at Kensington Town Hall in April 1993 on eating disorders, during which her more personable approach nearly resulted in a full-blown admission of her battle with bulimia. Diana had become a champion of women's issues by that time, having visited a refuge for domestic violence victims a month earlier. She also spoke at a conference in support of mentally ill women in June of that year.

But the whirlwind schedule, negative media attention, and other distractions began to catch up with Diana. She found herself depressed even before the events of 1994. She worried constantly about negative media coverage, which in turn kept her up at night. Diana even hired a sleep therapist, who regulated her intake of oxygen to provide a decent night's sleep. She was not only tired but also plagued by numbing headaches, all of which often put her in a foul mood. Diana grew angry and impatient with freelance photographers known as paparazzi, who followed her every move and sold their pictures to the highest bidder. She sought to escape, but rather than take the advice of those who suggested she whisk her children away to a quiet spot, Diana took them to Disney World. She figured on getting lost in the crowd, but she figured wrong. Photographers hounded her and her sons throughout the trip. When she returned to Kensington Palace, tabloid headlines criticized Diana for taking an expensive vacation overseas while spearheading charitable efforts to help starving children.

Another rocky wave in the stormy seas of Diana's life following the separation came courtesy of Prince Charles, who hired Alexandra "Tiggy" Legge-Bourke as a "surrogate mother" for William and Harry when they were not in Diana's care. The princess was angered at the sight of her younger son sitting on the knees of Legge-Bourke in newspaper photographs. Both Diana and Camilla disliked Legge-Bourke, who claimed that the princes needed what she was providing, such as a rifle and a horse, and not the tennis racket and bucket of popcorn at the movies offered by their mother. Diana not only considered her a threat to her motherhood, the only domain in which Charles and the royal family had yet to tamper, but grew to believe that she was having an affair with her estranged husband. Indeed, some at Buckingham Palace believed strongly that Legge-Bourke would make quite a suitable wife for the prince.

INVASION OF PRIVACY

One incident that November served to convince Diana to make dramatic changes in her public life. She opened up the *Sunday Mirror* one morning to see a full-page photograph of her working out in a tight leotard at a health club. Club manager Bryce Taylor was paid a handsome sum to hand the photos over to the newspaper. It was discovered that the picture had been taken without her knowledge with a camera secretly planted on the ceiling. It showed her on a rowing machine with her legs spread far apart. Diana sued the paper and settled before the case went to trial, ensuring that the photographs would never again be published. One might have expected a backlash against such media manipulation, but none was forthcoming, even after Taylor accused Diana of a secret desire to have such photos taken. The episode convinced Diana that the desire of the tabloid press to sell papers with little regard to the truth was stronger than her ability to prevent it. It also motivated Diana to make a resolution to withdraw from public life.

That decision was announced on December 3, 1993, during a Headway National Head Injuries Association gathering. Diana spoke emotionally and with conviction despite a trembling voice that asked for "time and space" before launching a further explanation. "When I started my public life 12 years ago, I understood that the media might be interested in what I did," she told those in attendance. "I realized then that their attention would inevitably focus on both our private and public lives. But I was not aware of how overwhelming that attention would become; nor the extent to which it would affect both my public duties and my personal life, in a manner that has been hard to bear."[4] She then spoke of her sons as her top priority before departing to a standing ovation.

With her public engagement schedule suddenly blank, Diana spent much of 1994 trying to find herself. She consulted various healers, astrologers, psychics, and other gurus in an effort to secure tranquility and fulfillment. She frequented masseurs and acupuncture specialists to heal her body. Paul Burrell noted Diana and astrologer Debbie Frank sitting on the carpet surrounded by zodiac charts while tracking the movements of the planets. "You really must have your chart read," Diana beseeched Burrell. "It's riveting stuff."[5] Yet though she felt strongly about the therapeutic benefits of such far-from-mainstream activities, Diana also showed an ability to laugh at them as well as herself for her involvement.

Psychotherapist Susie Orbach, a specialist in eating disorders who eventually tamed the bulimia from which Diana continued to suffer into the 1990s, performed one series of treatments on Diana. Orbach wrote a book in 1978 titled *Fat Is a Feminist Issue*, which claims that women's obsession with their weight is the result of men who control relationships. It's no wonder that Diana was fascinated with its contents—her desire to shed pounds was perpetuated by a need to look appealing enough to pry Charles away from Camilla. Though Diana developed a trusted friendship with healer Simone Simmons during the 1990s, Orbach proved to be her most important adviser. She not only helped Diana rid herself of her bulimia, but she also schooled her on developing a more positive relationship with Charles and the royal family. She even prepared Diana for a 1995 national television interview with *Panorama* reporter Martin Bashir.

Diana needed the help. Though she had been separated for nearly two years and had experienced relationships with other men, her anger toward Charles had not abated. When the prince claimed in his television interview with Dimbleby that he never loved her, she felt as strong an emotional pain as she had at any time during their 12 years together. And Diana was certainly far from over his relationship with Camilla. She confided to a friend that images in her mind of the two together during a drive on the highway resulted in feelings of jealous rage. "I felt mesmerized, unable to concentrate on anything but Charles and the bitch, Camilla," Diana said. "I could see them in my mind's eye kissing, making love, having a meal together, riding out together, listening to music together, doing everything together while I was alone with the boys taking them to school. I drove along with the tears welling in my eyes. But my heart was full of anger and hatred."[6]

Diana also had some choice words for Charles's admission that he had never loved her, not only in regard to herself but also to his sons. "How could he say something like that?" she asked. "Didn't he realize that was something terrible for the boys to hear about the relationship between their father and mother? Making that statement showed what a selfish prig Charles had become, as though nothing in the world matters, except his feelings—not his wife, his children, or any of their memories. I could gladly have scratched his eyes out for announcing that to the world."[7]

Shortly thereafter Camilla announced her pending divorce from Andrew Parker Bowles. It had been a marriage of convenience for quite some time anyway—he was quite aware of her relationship with Charles and had enjoyed no shortage of female companions of his own. But Diana felt that Camilla being single would allow her to freely display her love for the prince and spend more time with William and Harry. Soon it was publicly accepted that Camilla was Charles's mistress, which certainly destroyed any hope for a reconciliation of the royal marriage. Diana was summoned for a meeting with the queen and Prince Philip, who scolded the princess for her recent behavior and let it be known that she would be stripped of her title if it did not improve.

Her recent behavior included a relationship with hunky and quite married British rugby star Will Carling, who served as her unofficial personal trainer. Though neither admitted to physical encounters, various publications have insisted that the relationship was of a sexual nature. Carling's wife, Julia, told reporters that the princess was destroying her marriage, whereupon her husband vowed not to see Diana again. Soon thereafter, he was seen delivering rugby shirts to William and Harry at Kensington Palace, leading to the Carlings announcing their separation. Julia again approached the media with a finger of accusation pointed directly at Diana. In an autobiography written several years later, Will Carling refused to reveal the nature of his relationship with the princess. Many in the media assumed the two had engaged in sexual relations, and many still blamed Diana for the breakup of the marriage. *Today* asked, "Is Will Carling merely another trophy for the bored, manipulative and selfish princess?" while the *Daily Express* inquired, "Is no marriage and no man safe from the wife of the heir to the throne?"[8]

DIANA UNCENSORED

Diana insisted that her relationship with Carling had been platonic and that it had indeed ended when the story hit the tabloids, but her damaged reputation motivated her to plan a tell-all interview with Bashir on *Panorama*, the most respected news program on the British airwaves. An estimated 23 million British viewers tuned in to the interview, which ran on November 14, 1995—Prince Charles's 47th birthday. Diana candidly answered questions on a wide-ranging number of subjects, including those related to Charles, the royal family, her battles with bulimia, Gilbey, Hoare, and her duties as Princess of Wales. The following were highlights of the interview:

> On reaction to her postnatal depression: "It gave everybody a wonderful new label—Diana's unstable and Diana's mentally unbalanced. And unfortunately that seems to have stuck on and off over the years."
>
> On her bulimia: "You inflict it upon yourself because your self-esteem is at a low ebb, and you don't think you're worthy or valuable. . . . It was a symptom of what was going on in my marriage. I was crying out for help, but giving the wrong signals."
>
> On Camilla's role in the failure of her marriage: "Well, there were three of us in this marriage, so it was a bit crowded."
>
> On royal family treatment since the separation: "People's agendas changed overnight. I was now the separated wife of the Prince of Wales. I was a problem. I was a liability, and how are we going to deal with her?"

On her relationship with Hewitt: "He was a great friend of mine at a very difficult, yet another difficult time, and he was always there to support me, and I was absolutely devastated when this book appeared, because I trusted him. . . . There was a lot of fantasy in that book, and it was very distressing for me that a friend of mine, who I had trusted, made money out of me."

On whether she had been unfaithful to Charles: "Yes, I adored (Hewitt). Yes, I was in love with him."

On a typical day regarding paparazzi: "When I have my public duties, I understand that when I get out of the car I'm being photographed, but actually it's now when I get out of my door, my front door, I'm being photographed. I never know where a lens is going to be. A normal day would be followed by four cars, a normal day would be come back to my car and find six freelance photographers jumping around me."

On how she perceives her role: "The biggest disease this world suffers from in this day and age is the disease of people feeling unloved, and I know that I can give love for a minute, for half an hour, for a day, for a month, but I can give—I'm very happy to do that and I want to do that."[9]

The interview went over at Buckingham Palace like ripped jeans at a royal ball. Diana offered her view to Bashir that the royal family didn't allow her to grow as a person, that they gave her little credit for her performance, and that they undermined her role as Princess of Wales following the separation. Charles's private secretary, Dickie Arbiter, said the broadcast was received "like a cup of cold sick. We were gobsmacked, frankly. No one had seen it coming."[10] Even her mother, Frances Shand Kydd, whose relationship with the princess had admittedly soured, lambasted her daughter, calling the interview a "frightful mistake" and a "total error of judgment."[11]

The public took a quite different view. A *Daily Mirror* opinion poll revealed that an overwhelming 92 percent of those who responded supported Diana's statements during the interview. A national opinion poll sponsored by the *Sunday Times* showed that two-thirds of the British public lauded the interview, and a slightly higher percentage believed Diana should be presented with the role of goodwill ambassador abroad. The good graces by which she was viewed in her home country were cemented soon after the interview when she flew to the United States to receive a Humanitarian of the Year award from the United Cerebral

Palsy Foundation of New York. None other than former secretary of state Henry Kissinger presented the honor to her.

HER MEAN-SPIRITED SIDE

Perhaps the outpouring of public support made Diana feel invincible. That might explain her one-sided confrontation with Legge-Bourke during a staff Christmas lunch at the Lansborough Hotel on Hyde Park Corner upon her return from New York. She alerted Paul Burrell to watch her, then walked over to the nanny of her children, whom she suspected had become more than just an aide to Charles. "Hello, Tiggy. How are you?" Diana said, sporting a knowing smile. "*So sorry* to hear about the baby." The implication was that she had become pregnant with the prince's child and had it aborted. Legge-Bourke rushed from the room in horror, whereupon Diana turned to Burrell and said, "Did you see the look on her face, Paul? She almost fainted!"[12] Both Charles and the queen were furious. Diana's stinging allegations not only forced Legge-Bourke to contact lawyers to issue a statement denying them, but proved to be the last straw for the royal family in its acceptance of Diana and the current arrangement. An investigation revealed that Legge-Bourke had indeed visited her private gynecologist twice in the fall of 1995 and had also checked into a hospital, but nothing to indicate what the princess had charged. Diana was asked to apologize but refused. By that time, both Charles and the queen had insisted on a hastened divorce.

An outsider might suspect such a prospect would have Diana turning cartwheels. After all, three years had gone by since the separation and though she had yet to meet the man who would bring her fulfillment, she showed with certainty that she was open for exploration. Moreover, one would believe that her anger at Charles for his affair with Camilla and his admission on national television that he never loved her in the first place precluded any possibility that she wouldn't welcome a divorce. But those close to her believe strongly that Diana still loved Prince Charles and that she couldn't tolerate the finality of her relationship with him. Yes, she had threatened him with divorce on several occasions when they were together, but only so he would take notice of the issues in their marriage, primarily his infidelity.

But there it was—a letter from the queen herself, dated December 18, 1995, suggesting for the first time that Diana and Charles should divorce. It wasn't Diana's idea of acting in the Christmas spirit, but then the queen had seen enough of the media circus revolving around the extramarital affairs and petty bickering of both of them to allow it to continue. After all, she asked, what possible reason has either given for them to remain wed? The letter upset Diana, who complained to Burrell that the queen had discussed the issue with such officials as Prime Minister John Major and the archbishop of Canterbury before approaching her with it in such an impersonal manner as a letter from Windsor Castle. Under the circumstances, Diana cared little about the implications of her official breakup with Charles to the nation. Rather, how did it affect her and her sons? She believed such a personal, emotional subject should be handled in a personal, emotional manner, not as a business decision. The letter, however, was written with far from a businesslike approach. The queen simply pointed out that the damage already inflicted upon William and Harry could not be made any worse by a divorce.

Diana wasted no time phoning the queen, whom she politely attempted to convince to give the matter more thought, which was promised in return. The princess then penned a letter to the queen stating that she required more time. But the next day, a letter arrived from Charles stating flatly his request for a divorce, the inevitability of which he believed to be unquestionable. Curiously, a comparison of the prince's letter and that of the queen revealed passages that were identical, leading Diana to believe the plan for an immediate divorce had been hatched by both of them. She then scratched out a note to her estranged husband claiming her confusion and adding her refusal to agree to the divorce.

While fighting to keep her husband, at least officially, Diana lost private secretary P. D. Jephson, who stepped down in January 1996. He had been a loyal aide, but her callous remarks to Legge-Bourke along with word leaked to the press that the queen was calling for a divorce convinced Jephson that he could no longer remain with Diana. "My boss's treatment of Tiggy was all that my wavering resolve needed," Jephson wrote in his autobiography. "Later rather than sooner, I discovered that loyalty to the Princess *did* now conflict with a higher loyalty—namely to elementary decency. In the face of the Queen's letter urging divorce I also concluded that, if I was to stand up for the Princess as I should, I would inevitably be in conflict with the head of state."[13]

Media reports of the queen's letter sealed the fate of the royal marriage. Diana met with the queen in Buckingham Palace on February 15, 1996, the day after she sent a Valentine's Day card to Charles. Still plagued by jealousy, she asked the queen if she felt the prince was destined to marry Camilla, to which Diana received the welcome reply that it was quite unlikely. She told the queen flatly that she didn't want the divorce and that she was still in love with Charles, adding that she was blameless for the unfortunate situation. Diana believed that the queen and the Duke of Edinburgh had put forth great effort to preserve the marriage, but she didn't give the same credit to Charles. When they met to talk about the divorce two weeks later, she did, however, according to friends, tell her soon-to-be ex-husband that she would always love him.

Among the issues discussed was whether Diana would still be referred to as "Her Royal Highness." It was decided that her title would be "Diana, Princess of Wales." Diana claimed to friends she was insulted by the change in semantics, though Buckingham Palace officials insisted it was her idea. The divorce settlement gave Diana the equivalent of $2.2 million in a lump sum, as well as nearly $600,000 annually to run her office. She would still be considered a member of the royal family despite the loss of her title. The marriage was officially dissolved on August 28.

Diana was never one to fawn over money. Because she was raised in an aristocratic family and had grown accustomed to a royal life, the notion of being in financial need was foreign to her. But the notion of being in emotional need was all too familiar. It would remain with her to her death, a sorrowful event that proved tragically close.

NOTES

1. Nicholas Davies, *Diana: The Lonely Princess* (New York: Birch Lane Press, 1996), 54.

2. Ibid., 62.

3. Sarah Bradford, *Diana* (New York: Viking Press, 2006), 246.

4. Andrew Morton, *Diana: Her New Life* (New York: Simon and Schuster, 1994), 104.

5. Paul Burrell, *A Royal Duty* (New York: G. P. Putnam's Sons, 2003), 189.

6. Nicholas Davies, *Diana: The Lonely Princess* (New York: Birch Lane Press, 1996), 82–83.

7. Ibid.

8. Sally Bedell Smith, *Diana in Search of Herself* (New York: Times Books, 1999), 283.

9. Diana, Princess of Wales, interview by Martin Bashir, *Panorama*, BBC, November 20, 1995, http://www.bbc.co.uk/politics97/diana/panorama.html (accessed November 6, 2007).

10. Tina Brown, *The Diana Chronicles* (New York: Doubleday, 2007), 397.

11. Bradford, *Diana*, 296.

12. Burrell, *A Royal Duty*, 219.

13. P. D. Jephson, *Shadows of a Princess* (New York: HarperCollins, 2006), 447.

Chapter 12

THE FINAL YEARS
AND FATAL END

If Diana was suffering when the ink had barely dried on her divorce papers, she hid it quite well. In fact, friends and media members reported that she never looked or felt better. She feared that the finality of her marriage would overwhelm her emotionally; instead, it lifted her spirits and lightened her burden. In her most carefree moments, she claimed a disinterest in her former husband's relationship with Camilla and even expressed a hope that the two would wed because at least his former mistress would take good care of William and Harry.

Diana trimmed her staff considerably, which gave Paul Burrell multiple roles, including acting as a shoulder to cry on when necessary. But he wasn't needed in this role immediately following the divorce. She was looking for a clean break, which prompted another break—that of all her Princess of Wales china, which she smashed into pieces with a hammer. She then remarked that she could purchase anything with the money Charles was providing.

The princess also limited her charitable causes to the six about which she was most passionate—Centrepoint (for homeless young people), the Royal Marsden Hospital, the Great Ormond Street Hospital for children, the English National Ballet, the Leprosy Mission, and the National AIDS Trust. Aside from the ballet, which she adored on more of a personal level, Diana hoped to learn more about the needs of each charity without being perceived as a figurehead for the royal family. Reducing the number of charities in which she was involved allowed her to address those concerns in greater depth.

Meanwhile, Diana was busy strengthening friendships, the strongest of which was with president of Tiffany's Rosa Monckton, Brazilian ambassadress Lucia Flecha de Lima, and Lady Annabel Goldsmith, whom she considered a trusting mother figure. That trio provided Diana with close ties and allowed her to branch out socially. So did Cosima Somerset, who had recently broken up with husband Lord John Somerset and with whom Diana felt tremendous empathy due to their nearly identical experiences and cloudy outlooks at their futures.

In May 1996, Cosima received a rather frightening glimpse into Diana's daily battle with paparazzi. The two had taken an enlightening trip to Majorca, during which they bared their souls, discussing their lives from their childhoods to their divorces. As their hotel manager was chauffeuring them through the winding mountain roads, they were chased by paparazzi on cars and motorcycles. One pulled dangerously close to them and thrust his camera lens inches from the car window. Diana remained calm—she had become accustomed to such an attack on her privacy. Cosima was stunned not only at the nerve of the lone paparazzo, but at her friend's cool reaction to the incident.

The latest flame for Diana following her breakup with Charles was Pakistani heart surgeon Hasnat Khan. In fact, they spent the night together at Kensington Palace just hours after the divorce decree had been made official. She had known Khan for nearly a year at that point, but the media scrutiny and resulting backlash of her previous relationships motivated her to move slowly with Khan despite her adoration of him. Khan had been pursuing his PhD in London at the Brompton Hospital when he assisted in heart surgery for Joe Toffolo, the husband of Diana's acupuncturist. The princess, who had always been fascinated by the subject of medicine, was curious about Toffolo's condition and impending operation. That curiosity grew by leaps and bounds when Khan strode into the room and into her life. Her interest in him delved far deeper intellectually in comparison to her rather shallow relationships with Hewitt and Hoare. Khan had sparked in her an interest not only in Islam, to which she even considered converting, but also in spiritual matters regarding life and death. Diana often spent hours visiting patients in the hospital while waiting for Khan to finish work. She spent so much time with Khan at the hospital that she resorted to using a disguise, complete with a long, dark wig, in order to avoid attracting attention. The alias proved so effective that she began using it for everyday errands.

Diana eventually invited Hasnat to dinner at Kensington Palace to meet William and Harry. She was convinced that Hasnat was to be her life partner. For the first time, she had met a man who would be supportive of her and with whom she had developed a multidimensional relationship. But his independent nature precluded the closeness she required. Diana asked Hasnat to move into Kensington Palace, but he refused. He even rejected a mobile phone, which would have allowed Diana to reach him with the frequency she desired. Undeterred, she began leaving messages on his pager and calling the hospital switchboard with a phony name and urgency to reach him. Khan eventually tired of the charade, but it wasn't until the media finally caught wind of their relationship in November 1996 that Khan backed away. Ironically, it was her eagerness to further his career and begin their life together that proved their downfall. While in Italy to accept one of many humanitarian awards, Diana befriended Dr. Christian Barnard, who had performed the world's first heart transplant in 1967. She asked Barnard to find Khan work in South Africa, where they could start a home. The *Daily Mirror* soon revealed the relationship and Diana's yearning to be his wife.

A private person, Hasnat was angered by the publicity and unhappy with the princess for intruding on his professional life. He was further upset when Diana told *Daily Mail* reporter Richard Kay that the story was false despite the fact that she knew it to be true. Khan was also insulted that Diana would want to dismiss a story about her love for him. The episode motivated Khan to cut off communications with Diana for several weeks, which upset her terribly. Tears not shed since the divorce became official returned. The couple eventually reconciled, but not for long. Hasnat was discouraged by the inevitable publicity a relationship with Diana would entail. Diana continued her pursuit despite learning through friends of Hasnat's that if they did wed, she was destined to live with his family in Pakistan, where she would not have the responsibilities she'd grown accustomed to as a princess and she would be without the freedom that women in the Western culture take for granted. Even that didn't deter her. Her love for him clouded her judgment to such a degree that she flew to Pakistan in May 1997 to meet with his parents without his knowledge. His mother, Naheed, disapproved of her son's relationship with a glamorous British woman, while Hasnat himself was angered at Diana's actions and what he perceived as her attempts to control his life. The relationship was doomed.

NEW CAMPAIGN

The break from the royal family served to create two separate Dianas—the emotionally fragile woman who searched vainly, often with utter disregard for others, to find the ideal man and personal fulfillment, and the strong, caring princess who achieved humanitarian greatness by bringing hope and making positive changes to the lives of those less fortunate. Late in 1996 Director General of the British Red Cross Michael Whitlam began sending Diana photographs and reports regarding the devastation wrought by land mines planted during wartime that had never been cleared. Though Diana had eliminated the Red Cross as one of her charitable organizations, Whitlam believed the time was ripe for her to take on that cause. In mid-January 1997, she flew to the African nation of Angola. Fifteen million land mines had been scattered throughout the war-torn nation of just 12 million people, 70,000 of whom had stepped on one. The result was an estimated 40,000 amputees, with few having had their limbs replaced.

Upon her arrival in Angola, she immediately announced a campaign to help the Red Cross eliminate the use of antipersonnel land mines throughout the world, which ran contrary to official British policy, prompting criticism from Tory Party political figures. Diana was taken aback at the lack of appreciation for what she was attempting to accomplish, prompting Prime Minister John Major to express his support, claiming that the banning of land mines was in line with the ultimate objective of the British government. Diana gained further support when she was seen bravely trekking through minefields in the heavily mined town of Cuito. Asked jokingly by reporters to repeat the harrowing journey, she stunned all by complying. She also earned love and respect when she cheered specialists embarking on a dangerous mine-clearing mission and when, in typical Diana fashion, she comforted a child dying of injuries suffered in a land mine accident. She covered her up with a blanket, then spoke sweetly to her and stroked her hand. The child asked *Sunday Times* foreign correspondent Christina Lamb, "Who was that?" whereupon Lamb answered, "She's a princess from England, from far away." The child responded, "Is she an angel?" The child passed away from her wounds that afternoon.[1]

The mine controversy highlighted Diana's popularity and power. Her stand against land mines was supported not only by Labour Opposition leader Tony Blair and other liberals in the political landscape, but even by towering military figures such as U.S. general Norman Schwarzkopf and British counterpart Sir Peter de la Billiere. Diana had established herself as a humanitarian years earlier and was never one to concern herself with political matters. But her trip to Angola served to shake up British politics. Realizing the damage done by their criticizing of Diana for her support of a land mine ban, Tory officials scrambled to her side, but it was too late. A few months later, the party was thoroughly beaten in the general election, losing control of the government for the first time since 1979. The

44-year-old Blair took over as prime minister with the largest margin of victory in a British election in the twentieth century, signifying the blossoming of an era of youth, vitality, and new ideas in British politics. Diana was seen to fit in quite well with those ideals, and the land mine flap was considered a key ingredient in the ousting of the Tory government. "How dare anyone criticize Diana Princess of Wales for taking up this heartrending cause," wrote Secretary of State for International Development Clare Short. "Diana's stand on the issue deserves the utmost praise. Her public profile is able to give hope to millions of victims and campaigners that once and for all there may be a global ban on the manufacture and use of anti-personnel landmines."[2]

Meanwhile, it seemed Diana was stepping on an emotional land mine with every man she pursued. Her aggressiveness played a role in driving away Hasnat Khan, whose flattery at the notion of a beautiful princess falling in love with him was outweighed by his anger at her forays into his personal life and the resulting massive publicity. She accompanied the Khan family on an annual vacation to Stratford-on-Avon in June 1997, during which time it became obvious that her upbringing and background simply didn't allow her to fit in with the Muslim family. And when the affair between he and Diana was leaked to the media, Khan confided in a friend who suggested he end the relationship. Khan loved Diana, but in the end his mission in life was to become a doctor and take his skills back to his native Pakistan. When he informed Diana that it was over, her personal life had sunk to a new low. Though she had temporarily developed an acceptable postmarital relationship with Charles, with whom she got along well at events in which their children were involved, Diana no longer spoke to her mother. Frances not only had developed a drinking problem, but she had spoken out against her daughter's relationship with Khan due to his nationality and religion, whereupon the princess cut all ties with her. Frances sent letters of apology to Diana that were returned unopened.

She also grew distant from William and Harry, both of whom had embraced the rugged lifestyle supported by their father, Camilla, and Legge-Bourke. They preferred hunting and exploring the wilds or speeding around the go-kart track at Balmoral during their vacations from school to being hounded by the press at Disney World or hanging around the sprawling mansions owned by their mother's acquaintances. William in particular had developed a closeness with the royal family, especially the queen and the Duke of Edinburgh. He looked with great fervor at his destiny as the future king of England.

The thaw in Diana's relationship with Charles also took a hit. It ended when Mark Bolland, who had been hired in 1996 to improve the badly damaged public image of the prince, began working to cast Camilla in a favorable light. The prince's mistress had taken a financial battering after her divorce, which had been precipitated by Charles's public admission of an affair with her. Bolland decided that a positive public relations maneuver would be to have Charles finance Camilla's recovery, thereby showing responsibility toward the woman in his life. Camilla purchased a new home, complete with staff and a separate cottage for security provided by Scotland Yard. Charles covered much of the expense, including what amounted to an annual salary for Camilla. And when Charles selected Highgrove as the site of Camilla's 50th birthday bash on July 17, 1997, all of Diana's hatred and jealousy flooded back. After all, Charles now flaunted his love for the woman who had tormented the princess—in their former home, no less—while Diana could find no love at all. Bolland also arranged for a flattering television documentary about Camilla, which Diana couldn't help but watch despite the emotional pain she knew it would cause. The princess admitted her misery to astrologer and friend Debbie Frank after it aired.

LAST TANGO IN PARIS

As she did on several occasions to escape her anguish, Diana decided to take a trip. She accepted an invitation for herself and her sons to visit the home of Egyptian multimillionaire Mohammed Al-Fayed, wife Heini, and three of their youngest children in the South of France. The owner of Harrod's department store in London had known the Spencer family for years and was close friends with Diana's departed father and second wife Raine. Al-Fayed, who was fascinated by royalty and the lives they led, had learned through Raine about Diana's troubles. His invitation, which had originally been rejected, was offered simply to provide the princess peace of mind. She discovered upon her arrival that Al-Fayed had spent $15 million for a 200-foot yacht named the *Janikal* for the princess. And for company, he eventually provided eldest son Dodi, a carousing playboy and mildly noteworthy filmmaker with a well-publicized cocaine addiction who was engaged to marry American model Kelly Fisher.

Diana's initial impression of the Fayed family proved quite positive. Though she at one point chastised a horde of media members who had been tipped off about her trip, telling them in no uncertain terms to leave her alone, she thoroughly enjoyed jet-skiing and swimming with her sons and simply relaxing in Fayed's well-secured villa. But what she enjoyed most was getting to know Dodi, who had been romantically involved with not only Fisher, but well-known American models and actresses such as

Brooke Shields, Cathy Lee Crosby, and Julia Roberts. Though Dodi appeared to be a shallow hedonist on the surface, Diana explored his personality to uncover more. Among her findings was that Dodi had much in common with Charles, including a yearning for meaning in their lives and an inner sadness and sensitivity. Such vulnerability had always been attractive to Diana, who immediately took a liking to Dodi. And the feeling was mutual. Dodi not only displayed a genuine caring for the princess, but became a willing participant in her relationship with William and Harry. Dodi rented a disco for two nights so she and her sons could go dancing in private. The group also enjoyed a trip to a local amusement park, where they careened around in bumper cars. Diana appreciated that Dodi didn't appear to look at the boys as mere nuisances in his pursuit of her. The friendship many believe to be a necessary precursor to a loving relationship was achieved quickly.

But could Dodi have made Diana "the princess bride" again? Right-hand man Paul Burrell certainly didn't think so. He looked at Diana's feelings for the jet-setter as more of an infatuation than anything resembling love. She was swept away by his spontaneity and generosity. Soon after she returned from the South of France, Dodi asked her to fly to Paris for a dinner date. She called Burrell from her hotel suite brimming with excitement. She exclaimed with joy that Dodi had presented her with a beautiful gold watch surrounded by diamonds. And a week later, they returned to the *Janikal* for a Mediterranean cruise.

At the end of that fairy tale journey, Diana embarked on a humanitarian trip to the former Yugoslavia and Bosnia in a continuing effort to rid the world of antipersonnel land mines. During the excursion she befriended Americans Jerry White and Ken Rutherford, who founded the Landmine Survivors Network after they had become civilian victims of land mines. Of the two, only White had a leg remaining. As the group, which included Burrell and *Daily Telegraph* reporter Bill Deedes, drove toward Sarajevo, the two Americans spoke about their accidents, to which Diana offered, "My accident was on July 29, 1981," referring to her wedding. After a brief silence, the members of the group caught on to the joke and laughed heartily.[3]

Among the victims Diana visited in Sarajevo was a 15-year-old girl living with no parents in a miserable home. The girl had her leg blown off by an exploding land mine while she foraged through a pile of refuse for meager scraps of food for her two younger siblings. But as the media focused on that victim, the princess noticed the teenager's emaciated four-year-old sister lying on a foul-smelling mattress in the corner of a back room. The severely mentally retarded child was drenched in her own urine and her eyes were shut. Diana walked over, picked her up, cradled her, and stroked her arms and legs. The girl opened her eyes to reveal that she also had no pupils and was blind. "I witnessed something very special," Burrell wrote in his autobiography. "A simple act of humanity, an action that personi-fied the woman I knew so well."[4] Diana was scheduled to visit Cambodia and Vietnam that October, which would have given her another oppor-tunity to display her empathy toward the less fortunate and her hatred of land mines, which had taken so many lives. But her life was taken away before she would have the chance.

As Diana began her last three weeks on earth, it appeared that the prediction of her mother, which she had so violently scorned, was coming true. The loss of the title "Her Royal Highness" had indeed allowed her to experience personal growth and actually increase her importance. Diana's natural ability to communicate with others and her sincere concern for those in the world who desperately needed help were traits the loss of royal standing could not take away from her. And now she was free to pursue causes of interest to her and what she perceived as the most pressing is-sues for mankind. She was never fearful of taking controversial stands, and as only a nominal princess, Diana no longer had to concern herself with backlash. The British public remained so enamored with her that political figures rushed to her side in all her humanitarian efforts, as her stand on the elimination of land mines proved. Soon after her walk through the minefields of Angola, 122 nations agreed to ban antipersonnel land mines, and the campaign that her name and compassion brought into the world's spotlight was given a Nobel Peace Prize. Diana was ready to jump from her role as adored princess to vitally important international figure.

That is, until the wee hours of the morning of August 31, 1997.

CRASHING END TO THE LIFE OF A PRINCESS

As the previous day began, speculation about the depth of Diana's feel-ings toward Dodi remained in doubt. Though friend Simone Simmons claimed the princess never felt romantically close to Dodi and believed that the two didn't consummate their relationship, Diana told friends that she adored him and that Dodi had brought her true happiness. But any rela-tionship in which the princess was involved brought out the tabloid report-ers. The paparazzi followed the couple, particularly while they lounged on the 200-foot yacht. Diana didn't mind on those particular occasions. After all, how bothersome could having her picture taken from hundreds of feet away be? And she didn't mind that pictures of her relaxing on the *Janikal* appeared in newspapers all over the world. They showed her in a serene and content state. It was when the paparazzi hounded her and invaded her space that Diana was truly angered.

The couple was planning on staying at Dodi's apartment that night in Paris after spending time in the Imperial Suite of the Ritz. Dodi's personal chauffeur, Philippe Dourneau, was whisking them away from the hotel in a Mercedes limousine, which was followed by two security guards in a Range Rover. They reached their destination, only to be forced to struggle through a mob of paparazzi to get to the front door of Dodi's apartment building. Two hours later, they left for their dinner plans at fancy Chez Benoit and again were harassed by paparazzi. Dodi was so disturbed by the throng that he instructed his chauffeur to drive them back to the Ritz. Upon their arrival, cameras were thrust within inches of Diana's face. Though annoyed, she had become accustomed to such invasions of her privacy. Dodi, however, was shaken by the experience. The attention they drew once inside the restaurant motivated them to eat their meal upstairs in their suite. That's when Dodi created a plan to rid themselves of the paparazzi. He would order the limo and Range Rover drivers to start their engines, thereby tricking the paparazzi into believing they would be leaving out the front door while they actually departed through the back door into another car.

The maneuver didn't have its desired effect. Though most of the paparazzi indeed waited out front, a few maintained their positions behind the Ritz. At 12:20 AM, Diana and Dodi jumped into the backseat of a rented Mercedes that had pulled up. In the front seats were bodyguard Trevor Rees-Jones and driver Henri Paul, an assistant security director at the Ritz who screamed at the paparazzi, "Don't bother following—you won't catch us."[5] With paparazzi in cars and motorcycles giving chase, the Mercedes traveled at speeds estimated from 90 to 122 miles per hour into the Alma Tunnel, which has a posted speed limit of 30 miles per hour. Seconds later, the Mercedes crashed into a pillar, then spun across two lanes into a wall, tossing the passengers violently. The first to arrive at the crash scene was 25-year-old paparazzo Romuald Rat, who leaped from his vehicle, aimed his camera at the tangled, twisted wreck, and snapped three pictures that he would sell to the *Sun* as a one-day exclusive for nearly $500,000. Rat opened the rear car door of the Mercedes and realized immediately that Dodi and Paul were dead. Rees-Jones, the only passenger who had worn a seat belt, had survived multiple wounds. Diana was doubled over with her head stuck between the two front seats, barely breathing. Soon other photographers arrived as flashbulbs lit up the night. French photographer Christian Martinez began taking pictures inside the Mercedes, prompting his rival Rat to scream at him to stop taking pictures of such a gruesome scene. Martinez shouted vulgarities at Rat, then yelled, "Get out of the way! I'm doing the same job as you!"[6]

The car was crushed. The grille had been smashed two-thirds of the way back toward the dashboard, and the roof had been smashed to seat level. French physician Frederick Mailliez came upon the accident and immediately called for an ambulance from his car phone. He rushed to the 36-year-old Diana, who was then unconscious. Mailliez was surrounded by about a dozen photographers who had gathered to take pictures of the scene, none of whom offered to help. A police officer rescued one lone paparazzo who was being beaten by indignant onlookers. It took two hours to extract the princess from the wreckage, whereupon she was taken to Pitie Salpetriere Hospital, where doctors worked in vain for two hours to save her life. Diana suffered from severe wounds to her lung, head, and thigh and died from cardiac rest at 4:00 AM.

The catastrophic news was met with shock and grief throughout the world. Thousands gathered at the hospital after Diana's death was announced. Among the first to offer condolences was French prime minister Lionel Jospin, who expressed sorrow that the tragedy took place in his country. "It was so sad that this beautiful young woman, loved by everyone, whose every act and gesture were scrutinized, ended her life tragically in France, in Paris," he said. "Since the French were always seduced by her charm, I wanted to make a gesture."[7] Sporting events such as professional soccer matches in Britain were immediately cancelled. That nation experienced a period of profound bereavement as new prime minister Tony Blair spoke for his countrymen. "We are today a nation in Britain in a state of shock, in mourning, in grief so deeply painful for us," Blair said. "We know how difficult things were for her from time to time. I am sure we can only guess that. But people everywhere, not just here in Britain, kept faith with Princess Diana. . . . She was the people's princess and that is how she will stay, how she will remain in our hearts and memories forever."[8] By early morning, thousands began gathering outside both her Kensington Palace home and Buckingham Palace. Many left single flowers or bouquets. One little girl who appeared no older than three left a bright yellow, wounded teddy bear. Soon Diana's flag-draped coffin was loaded into a vehicle outside the hospital for transport to Villacoublay Airfield and a trip back to London.

GOODBYE, DIANA

Diana's coffin was carried from the Kensington Palace gates to the center of London in a solemn 105-minute procession. It eventually arrived at Westminster Abbey, where British monarchs have historically been buried. More than a million people lined the streets, the largest crowd gathered in that nation since a far more joyous occasion in 1945—the German surrender that marked the end of World War II. Prince Charles, sons William and Harry, the Duke of Edinburgh, and Diana's brother Charles Spencer joined the procession. Pop singer Elton John caused an outpouring of emotion and a flood of tears by playing on piano a sorrowful rendition of "Candle in the Wind," originally written for Marilyn Monroe. The song's lyrics, rewritten for the occasion, began "Goodbye, England's Rose." The highlight of the funeral, which was shown on two huge screens in Hyde Park, was an angry yet eloquent and touching eulogy by Diana's brother. He described the princess as "the most hunted person of the modern age" and referred to the paparazzi as being "at the opposite end of the moral spectrum" from his sister.[9]

In the days following the funeral, which was watched by an estimated 2.5 billion television viewers in 187 countries, the actions of the paparazzi were severely criticized. Steve Coz, editor of noted American gossip tabloid the *National Enquirer,* reported soon after the accident that paparazzi who took photos of the death scene were expecting to make up to $1 million. Coz also noted that the tabloids had engaged in a bidding war for the first picture showing Dodi and the princess kissing. "To a paparazzo," Coz said, "that's like waving a lottery ticket. This was a tragedy waiting to happen."[10]

Tragic, yes. But others believed such a disaster could have been avoided had Diana taken a stronger stand against the paparazzi years earlier. *Daily Mirror* reporter James Whitaker, who admitted to shedding tears as he penned his story about her death, was among those who felt the princess had for far too long and for her own benefit used media members, even those as shady as the paparazzi who followed her. Whitaker offered the recent trip with Dodi to the French Riviera as an example. "She walked on the beach, she got on a jet ski, she got on a motorboat," Whitaker explained. "Why shouldn't she do this? I'm not saying she shouldn't. But that was definitely a virtuoso performance for us to get photographs and a story. It's terrible what happened, but there's an element of use of the paparazzi and photographers in general that Diana used enormously to her advantage."[11]

Though the furor over the paparazzi remained heated, tests that revealed that driver Henri Paul was legally drunk shifted the blame. Paul's blood alcohol level was three times the legal limit, and he had consumed the alcohol along with Tiapride and anti-depressant Prozac, prescription drugs that come with explicit warnings against combining with alcohol.

The circumstances surrounding the accident mattered a great deal to many in Britain, but far more to 15-year-old William and 12-year-old Harry, who had been vacationing with their father in Scotland when the story broke. They knew only that their mother was gone forever. One of the three wreaths that rested on her casket simply read, "Mummy." Diana's sons held in their emotions through much of the ordeal, but broke into tears as they walked behind her coffin as it made its journey to Westminster Abbey. William appeared especially distraught. Diana looked upon him as not only a son but an adviser and friend.

Charles had had the unenviable task of informing his sons that their mother was dead. Upon hearing the news, the grief-stricken prince took a walk alone around Balmoral. He felt a myriad of emotions, including guilt. Had he not been unfaithful, perhaps the marriage would have continued and Diana would have seen no need to find comfort in the arms of other men. Charles was also consumed by the effect her passing would have on William and Harry, whom he proceeded to give the horrific news. William had confronted his mother about what he perceived to be an unhealthy relationship with Dodi; now he would never have the opportunity to apologize. Harry was overwhelmed with sadness and a sense of loss. He would never again experience the comfort and joy of cuddling with his mother on the couch and watching videos.

And, tragically, Diana would never again provide her magic touch to the billions who needed it most. During the procession in which the body of the princess was taken to Westminster Abbey, hundreds of people representing the charities she embraced joined the solemn march. It was no longer a royal ceremony; it was a moving display of Diana's tremendous worth to the world. People with AIDS, victims of land mines, and advocates for the homeless—they all walked to show their love for Diana.

There was much to love. The little girl who cared for her furry animals had blossomed into a woman who cared for the world.

NOTES

1. Tina Brown, *The Diana Chronicles* (New York: Doubleday, 2007), 427.

2. Tina Brown, "The Real Diana," RD.com, August 2007, http://www.rd.com/content/the-real-princess-diana/7/ (accessed November 12, 2007).

3. Paul Burrell, *A Royal Duty* (New York: G. P. Putnam's Sons, 2003), 285.

4. Ibid., 286.

5. Sally Bedell Smith, *Diana in Search of Herself* (New York: Times Books, 1999), 356.

6. Brown, *The Diana Chronicles*, 443.

7. Anne Swardson and Charles Trueheart, "An Outpouring of Sorrow, Love at Crash Site and Hospital," *Washington Post*, September 1, 1997, A28.

8. Dan Balz, "World Mourns Death of the 'People's Princess,'" *Washington Post*, September 1, 1997, A1.

9. Dan Balz, "Sorrowful Farewell to the 'People's Princess,'" *Washington Post*, September 7, 1997, A1.

10. Bruce Wallace, "Diana, Princess of Wales," *Maclean's*, September 8, 1997, 28–32.

11. Ibid.

EPILOGUE

As months and years passed, both ridiculous and valid conspiracy theories found their way into the mass media. At one point, more than 35,000 Web sites were dedicated to mostly frivolous hypotheses claiming that Diana's death was planned. Bitter Mohamed Al-Fayed asserted that Prince Philip had the princess murdered because she was soon to marry an Egyptian Muslim who would then become the half brother of the heir to the throne. "Prince Philip is the one responsible for giving the order [to have Diana killed]," Al-Fayed claimed. "He is very racist. He is of German blood, and I'm sure he is a Nazi sympathizer."[1]

Every investigation into the crash concluded that Al-Fayed's allegations were unfounded. A three-year inquiry aggressively pursued by former Metropolitan Police chief Lord Stevens, dubbed Operation Paget, resulted in the dismissal of every claim brought forth by Al-Fayed and the media. Research by French officials reached the same verdict. Among the charges were that someone had flashed a light in Paul's eyes to blind him while he was driving, that the royal family wanted Diana murdered because she was pregnant with Dodi's baby, and that a driver in a Fiat Uno had purposely sideswiped the Mercedes to cause an accident. The driver of the Fiat Uno was Le Van Thanh, a Vietnamese plumber. He did repaint his car red after the accident, but only to avoid prosecution under French law, which stipulates the illegality of leaving the scene of an accident even when not involved.

While the majority of the British and the world public either lost interest in the case or simply accepted that Diana's death was the result of an accident, Al-Fayed continued to insist that Prince Philip ordered the murders of the princess and his son and had British security operatives carry it out. What appeared to be the last hope for Al-Fayed to have his theory proved was being carried out just after the 10th anniversary of the accident in late 2007. Lord Justice Scott Baker, who was serving as the coroner in the case, asked a jury in early October to determine the cause of death. Though no individual could be implicated in the case, the jury of six women and five men had the freedom to rule that it was a murder plot. That scenario, however, appeared quite unlikely. Neither Queen Elizabeth II nor Prince Charles were scheduled to testify, much to the dismay of Al-Fayed, who believed their insight would prove his contention. Fayed even stretched his theory to include that Diana and Dodi were going to announce their engagement on September 1, the day after the crash.

Life, however, goes on. Following the death of Princess Diana, Charles asked the media to respect the privacy of sons William and Harry. He hoped the same tabloids that played a role in the crash that stole the life of their mother would allow the princes to grieve privately and concentrate on their educations without great fanfare.

William, who is second in line to the throne behind his father, excelled in various subjects, including geography, biology, and art history, at Eton College, before taking a year off to visit Chile, toil on British dairy farms, and tour Africa. He then moved on to study at St. Andrews University in Scotland, where he concentrated on geography and graduated in 2005. Soon thereafter he joined the Royal Military Academy Sandhurst as an officer cadet and was eventually commissioned as an army officer. He quickly latched on as a second lieutenant with the Household Cavalry.

Harry has led a more controversial life since the accident that took his mother away. He followed William to Eton in 1998 and also spent time traveling to Australia, Argentina, and Africa. It was on that final trip during which he created a well-received documentary on the plight of orphans in Lesotho. Harry found quite the opposite reaction when he wore a swastika armband at a costume party in January 2005. The 20-year-old prince apologized profusely for what he described as a poor choice. The incident caused quite a stir, but eventually blew over under the realization that it in no way reflected his political views. Harry soon thereafter followed in his brother's footsteps by entering the Royal Military Academy Sandhurst and undergoing nearly a year of training as an officer cadet. He too was commissioned as a second lieutenant in the Household Cavalry in 2006.

Neither son, however, has distanced himself emotionally from Diana. In fact, William and Harry organized a tribute memorial concert in her name to recognize the 10th anniversary of her death. The event was broadcast in 140 different countries and reached 500 million homes. About 22,500 tickets were made available for the concert in December 2006 and were snapped up in 17 minutes. A throng of 63,000 attended the July 2007 concert at Wembley Stadium, where artists such as Elton John, Sir Tom Jones, Duran Duran, Andrea Bocelli, Rod Stewart, and Kanye West performed. Speeches by both princes, as well as former and current world leaders such as Bill Clinton, Nelson Mandela, and Tony Blair, highlighted the festivities, which reached a crescendo when a video tribute to Diana was shown.

One celebrity who did not attend the concert was Prince Charles. Many in Britain still considered him a villain 10 years after Diana's death, offering that if he had given all his affection to his wife rather than to Camilla, the princess wouldn't have felt it necessary to search for love elsewhere and would still be alive. Charles strengthened his relationship with William and Harry following the death of their mother. They accompanied him on several trips both inside Britain and abroad.

Charles didn't lose his feelings for Camilla after the tragedy. The couple married in a civil ceremony in Windsor on April 9, 2005. After the wedding, which was attended by 800 guests and was followed by a reception hosted by the queen, Camilla assumed the title of Her Royal Highness, the Duchess of Cornwall. The couple traveled together on official visits to the United States in 2005, the Middle East and Western Asia in 2006, and both the United States and the Middle East in 2007. The visits took on quite a different flavor and atmosphere than those undertaken by Charles and Diana, particularly in the last several years of their marriage. The insults and petty bickering that marred the official engagements of Prince Charles and Princess Diana were replaced by the respect the new royal couple felt for each other, and the adoring crowds that besieged Diana wherever she went have been replaced by a quieter existence. But the legacy of Diana, Princess of Wales, endures as her sons and those who knew her continue to keep her memory alive.

NOTE

1. Tina Brown, The Diana Chronicles (New York: Doubleday, 2007), 459.

SELECTED BIBLIOGRAPHY

Bradford, Sarah. *Diana*. New York: Viking Press, 2006.

Brown, Tina. *The Diana Chronicles*. New York: Doubleday, 2007.

Burrell, Paul. *A Royal Duty*. New York: G. P. Putnam's Sons, 2003.

Clayton, Tim, and Phil Craig. *Diana: Story of a Princess*. New York: Simon and Schuster, 2001.

Coward, Rosalind. *Diana: The Portrait*. Riverside, N.J.: Andrews McMeel Publishing, 2004.

Davies, Nicholas. *Diana: The Lonely Princess*. New York: Birch Lane Press, 1996.

Dimbleby, Jonathan. *The Prince of Wales: A Biography*. London: Little, Brown and Company, 1993.

Jephson, P. D. *Shadows of a Princess*. New York: HarperCollins, 2006.

Junor, Penny. *The Firm, The Troubled Life of the House of Windsor*. New York: St. Martin's Press, 2005.

Kurz, Martine, and Christine Gaughey. *Diana: A Princess for the World*. Paris: Editions de la Martiniere, 1997.

Martin, Ralph G. *Charles & Diana*. Boston: G. K. Hall, 1986.

Morton, Andrew. *Diana: Her New Life*. New York: Simon and Schuster, 1994.

———. *Diana: Her True Story*. New York: Simon and Schuster, 1997.

Mulvaney, Jay. *Diana and Jackie*. New York: St. Martin's Press, 2002.

Pasternak, Anne. *Princess in Love* (paperback). New York: Penguin USA, 1994.

Simmons, Simone. *Diana: The Last Word*. New York: St. Martin's Press, 2005.

Smith, Sally Bedell. *Diana in Search of Herself*. New York: Times Books, 1999.

WEB SITES

Time magazine coverage of Princess Diana by Howard Chua-Eoan: http://www.time.com/daily/special/diana/

"Diana, Princess of Wales": http://www.royal.gov.uk/output/Page151.asp

"The Death of Princess Diana," CNN: www.cnn.com/SPECIALS/1998/08/diana

"Princess Diana—Diana, Princess of Wales": www.princess.diana.com/diana/diana.php

"Coroner's Inquests into the Deaths of Diana, Princess of Wales and Mr. Dodi Al Fayed": http://www.scottbaker-inquests.gov.uk/

INDEX

About the Author

MARTIN GITLIN is a freelance book writer and journalist based in Cleveland, Ohio. He has written several history books for students, including works on the landmark *Brown v. Board of Education* case, Battle of The Little Bighorn and Stock Market Crash of 1929. He has also written biographies of NASCAR drivers Jimmie Johnson and Jeff Gordon. Gitlin worked for two decades as a sportswriter, during which time he won more than 45 awards, including first place for general excellence from Associated Press. That organization also selected him as one of the top four feature writers in Ohio.